# Kool kid Food

quick 'n' easy **kids'** foods

# Contents

# Breakfast & Lunch Fun

Get the kids going with a fun breakfast or jumping into high gear with one of these great lunches.

 **Super Easy** Berry Good Dip

8 ounces fresh or thawed frozen strawberries
4 ounces nonfat cream cheese, softened
¼ cup reduced-fat sour cream
1 tablespoon sugar

**1.** Place strawberries in food processor or blender container; process until smooth.

**2.** Beat cream cheese in small bowl until smooth. Stir in sour cream, strawberry purée and sugar; cover. Refrigerate until ready to serve.

**3.** Spoon dip into small serving bowl. Garnish with orange peel, if desired. Serve with assorted fresh fruit dippers or angel food cake cubes.

*Makes 6 (¼-cup) servings*

**Little Helpers**

For a super quick fruit spread for toasted mini English muffins or bagels, beat 1 package (8 ounces) softened nonfat cream cheese in a small bowl until fluffy. Stir in 3 to 4 tablespoons strawberry spreadable fruit. Season to taste with 1 to 2 teaspoons sugar, if desired. Makes 6 servings.

# Creamy Cinnamon Rolls

**2 (1-pound) loaves frozen bread dough, thawed**
**⅔ cup (one-half 14-ounce can) EAGLE® BRAND Sweetened**
    **Condensed Milk (NOT evaporated milk), divided\***
**1 cup chopped pecans**
**2 teaspoons ground cinnamon**
**1 cup sifted powdered sugar**
**½ teaspoon vanilla extract**
    **Additional chopped pecans (optional)**

*\*Use remaining Eagle Brand as a dip for fruit. Pour into storage container and store tightly covered in refrigerator for up to 1 week.*

**1.** On lightly floured surface, roll each of bread dough loaves to 12×9-inch rectangle. Spread ⅓ cup Eagle Brand over dough rectangles. Sprinkle with 1 cup pecans and cinnamon. Roll up jelly-roll style starting from a short side. Cut each into 6 slices.

**2.** Generously grease 13×9-inch baking pan. Place rolls cut sides down in pan. Cover loosely with greased waxed paper and then with plastic wrap. Chill overnight. Cover and chill remaining Eagle Brand.

**3.** To bake, let pan of rolls stand at room temperature for 30 minutes. Preheat oven to 350°F. Bake 30 to 35 minutes or until golden brown. Cool in pan 5 minutes; loosen edges and remove rolls from pan.

**4.** Meanwhile for frosting, in small bowl, combine powdered sugar, remaining ⅓ cup Eagle Brand and vanilla. Drizzle frosting on warm rolls. Sprinkle with additional chopped pecans. *Makes 12 rolls*

**Prep Time:** 20 minutes
**Bake Time:** 30 to 35 minutes
**Chill Time:** overnight
**Cool Time:** 5 minutes

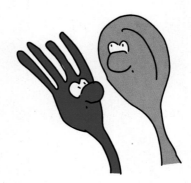

*Creamy Cinnamon Roll*

 **Super Easy** ## Snacking Surprise Muffins

1½ **cups all-purpose flour**
½ **cup sugar**
1 **cup fresh or frozen blueberries**
2½ **teaspoons baking powder**
1 **teaspoon ground cinnamon**
¼ **teaspoon salt**
1 **egg, beaten**
⅔ **cup buttermilk**
¼ **cup margarine or butter, melted**
3 **tablespoons peach preserves**

**TOPPING**
1 **tablespoon sugar**
¼ **teaspoon ground cinnamon**

**1.** Preheat oven to 400°F. Line 12 medium muffin cups with paper liners; set aside.

**2.** Combine flour, ½ cup sugar, blueberries, baking powder, 1 teaspoon cinnamon and salt in medium bowl. Combine egg, buttermilk and margarine in small bowl. Add to flour mixture; mix just until moistened.

**3.** Spoon about 1 tablespoon batter into each muffin cup. Drop a scant teaspoonful of preserves into center of batter in each cup; top with remaining batter.

**4.** Combine 1 tablespoon sugar and ¼ teaspoon cinnamon in small bowl; sprinkle evenly over tops of batter.

**5.** Bake 18 to 20 minutes or until lightly browned. Remove muffins to wire rack to cool completely. *Makes 12 servings*

**Little Helpers**

Cool muffins on a wire rack until they are cool enough to eat. They are best when served warm. Store in an airtight plastic bag for several days. For longer storage, wrap and freeze.

*Snacking Surprise Muffins*

# Banana Pancakes

   1  **cup all-purpose flour**
   1  **tablespoon sugar**
   1  **teaspoon baking powder**
   ½  **teaspoon baking soda**
   ½  **teaspoon salt**
   1  **container (6 ounces) banana custard-style yogurt**
   ½  **cup skim milk**
   1  **egg, beaten**
   2  **tablespoons vegetable oil**
   1  **cup cooked rice**
   1  **cup puréed or finely diced banana**
      **Vegetable cooking spray**

Combine flour, sugar, baking powder, baking soda and salt in large bowl. Add yogurt, milk, egg and oil; stir until smooth. Stir in rice and banana. Pour ¼ cup batter onto hot griddle coated with cooking spray. Cook over medium heat until bubbles form on top and underside is lightly browned. Turn to brown other side. Continue with remaining batter.          *Makes 12 (4-inch) pancakes*

*Favorite recipe from* **USA Rice Federation**

# Breakfast Hash

   1  **pound BOB EVANS® Special Seasonings or Sage Roll Sausage**
   2  **cups chopped potatoes**
   ¼  **cup chopped red and/or green bell pepper**
   2  **tablespoons chopped onion**
   6  **eggs**
   2  **tablespoons milk**

Crumble sausage into large skillet. Add potatoes, peppers and onion. Cook over low heat until sausage is browned and potatoes are fork-tender, stirring occasionally. Drain off any drippings. Whisk eggs and milk in small bowl until blended. Add to sausage mixture; scramble until eggs are set but not dry. Serve hot. Refrigerate leftovers.          *Makes 6 to 8 servings*

**Serving Suggestion:** Serve with fresh fruit.

# Country Chicken Pot Pie

  **1  package (1.8 ounces) white sauce mix**
**2¼  cups milk**
  **2  to 3 cups diced cooked chicken***
  **3  cups BIRDS EYE® frozen Mixed Vegetables**
**1½  cups seasoned croutons****

*\*No leftover cooked chicken handy? Before beginning recipe, cut 1 pound boneless skinless chicken into 1-inch cubes. Brown chicken in 1 tablespoon butter or margarine in large skillet, then proceed with recipe.*

*\*\*For a quick homemade touch, substitute 4 bakery-bought biscuits for croutons. Split and add to skillet, cut side down.*

• Prepare white sauce mix with milk in large skillet according to package directions.

• Add chicken and vegetables. Bring to boil over medium-high heat; cook 3 minutes or until heated through, stirring occasionally.

• Top with croutons; cover and let stand 5 minutes.

*Makes about 4 servings*

**Serving Suggestion:** Serve with a green salad.

**Prep Time:** 5 minutes
**Cook Time:** 15 minutes

### Little Helpers

Helping to cook should be safe as well as fun. Always wash your hands with hot soapy water before handling and preparing food. Rewash hands after touching your nose or mouth.

# Hot Dog Macaroni

1 package (8 ounces) hot dogs
1 cup uncooked corkscrew pasta
1 cup shredded Cheddar cheese
1 box (10 ounces) BIRDS EYE® frozen Green Peas
1 cup 1% milk

• Slice hot dogs into bite-size pieces; set aside.

• In large saucepan, cook pasta according to package directions; drain and return to saucepan.

• Stir in hot dogs, cheese, peas and milk. Cook over medium heat 10 minutes or until cheese is melted, stirring occasionally.          *Makes 4 servings*

**Prep Time:** 10 minutes
**Cook Time:** 20 minutes

# Salami Burger

1 teaspoon parve margarine
1 (12-ounce) HEBREW NATIONAL® Beef Salami or Lean Beef
    Salami Chub, thinly sliced
6 hard rolls or sesame seed buns, split, toasted
    HEBREW NATIONAL® Deli Mustard
3 medium tomatoes, thinly sliced
6 lettuce leaves

Melt margarine in large nonstick skillet over medium heat. Add salami; cook until heated through. Spread insides of rolls with mustard. Layer salami, tomatoes and lettuce inside rolls.          *Makes 6 servings*

# Campbell's® Chicken with a Twist

1 can (10¾ ounces) **CAMPBELL'S® Condensed Cheddar Cheese Soup**

¼ cup **milk**

1 cup **PACE® Picante Sauce** *or* **Thick & Chunky Salsa**

½ teaspoon **garlic powder** *or* **2 cloves garlic, minced**

1 can (about 8 ounces) **whole kernel corn, drained**

1½ cups **cubed cooked chicken** *or* **turkey**

4 cups **cooked corkscrew macaroni (3 cups uncooked)**

In large saucepan mix soup, milk, picante sauce, garlic powder, corn, chicken and macaroni. Over low heat, heat through.         *Makes 4 servings*

**Tip:** No cooked chicken on hand? Substitute 2 cans (5 ounces *each*) SWANSON® Premium Chunk Chicken Breast *or* Chunk Chicken for 1½ cups cooked chicken.

**Prep Time:** 5 minutes
**Cook Time:** 20 minutes

### Little Helpers

Be smart with your leftovers. Any food remaining after the meal should be stored within 2 hours of serving. Leftover foods can be wrapped in plastic or foil, then sealed inside plastic bags and frozen, if desired. Plastic bags can take up less freezer space than rigid containers.

## Kids' Wrap

4 teaspoons Dijon honey mustard
2 (8-inch) fat-free flour tortillas
2 slices reduced-fat American cheese, torn into halves
4 ounces fat-free oven-roasted turkey breast
½ cup shredded carrots (about 1 medium)
3 romaine lettuce leaves, washed and torn into bite-size pieces

**1.** Spread 2 teaspoons mustard evenly over one tortilla.

**2.** Top with 2 cheese halves, half of turkey, half of shredded carrots and half of torn lettuce.

**3.** Roll up tortilla and cut in half. Repeat with remaining ingredients.

*Makes 2 servings*

## Pizza Burger

1 pound lean ground beef
1 cup (4 ounces) shredded mozzarella cheese
1 tablespoon minced onion
1½ teaspoons chopped fresh oregano *or* ½ teaspoon dried oregano leaves
1 tablespoon chopped fresh basil *or* 1 teaspoon dried basil leaves
½ teaspoon salt
Dash black pepper
Prepared pizza sauce, heated
English muffins

Preheat grill. Combine ground beef, cheese, onion, oregano, basil, salt and pepper in medium bowl; mix lightly. Shape into four patties.

Grill 8 minutes or to desired doneness, turning once. Top with pizza sauce. Serve on English muffins. *Makes 4 servings*

## Broccoli-Cheese Quesadillas

> 1 cup (4 ounces) shredded nonfat Cheddar cheese
> ½ cup finely chopped fresh broccoli
> 2 tablespoons picante sauce or salsa
> 4 (6- to 7-inch) corn or flour tortillas
> 1 teaspoon margarine, divided

**1.** Combine cheese, broccoli and picante sauce in small bowl; mix well.

**2.** Spoon ¼ of the cheese mixture onto 1 side of each tortilla; fold tortilla over filling.

**3.** Melt ½ teaspoon margarine in 10-inch nonstick skillet over medium heat. Add 2 quesadillas; cook about 2 minutes on each side or until tortillas are golden brown and cheese is melted. Repeat with remaining margarine and quesadillas. Cool completely.

*Makes 4 servings*

> **Tip**
> Refrigerate individually wrapped quesadillas up to 2 days or freeze up to 3 weeks.

## Saucy Chicken

> 2 pounds chicken breasts
> 1 (8-ounce) bottle Russian or French salad dressing
> 1 (1.25-ounce) envelope onion soup mix (dry)
> 1 cup (12-ounce jar) SMUCKER'S® Apricot Preserves
> Hot cooked rice

Place chicken skin-side-up in 13×9-inch baking pan. Combine dressing, soup mix and preserves; mix well. Pour over chicken.

Bake at 350° for 1 hour or until chicken is fork-tender and juices run clear; halfway through cooking time, spoon sauce over breasts. Serve over hot cooked rice.

*Makes 8 servings*

*Broccoli-Cheese Quesadilla*

## Sub on the Run

2 (2 ounces each) hard rolls, split into halves
4 tomato slices
14 turkey pepperoni slices
2 ounces fat-free oven-roasted turkey breast
¼ cup (1 ounce) shredded part-skim mozzarella or reduced-fat sharp Cheddar cheese
1 cup packaged coleslaw mix or shredded lettuce
¼ medium green bell pepper, thinly sliced (optional)
2 tablespoons prepared fat-free Italian salad dressing

Top each of the two bottom halves of rolls with 2 tomato slices, 7 pepperoni slices, half of turkey, 2 tablespoons cheese, ½ cup coleslaw mix and half of bell pepper slices, if desired. Drizzle with salad dressing. Top with roll tops. Cut into halves, if desired. *Makes 2 servings*

 ## Prego® Pronto Pizza

¾ cup PREGO® Traditional Pasta Sauce or Extra Chunky Tomato, Onion & Garlic Pasta Sauce
1 Italian bread shell (about 16 ounces)
1½ cups shredded mozzarella cheese (6 ounces)

Preheat oven to 425°F. Spread pasta sauce over shell to edge. Top with cheese. Bake 12 minutes or until cheese is melted. *Makes 4 servings*

**Prep Time:** 10 minutes
**Cook Time:** 12 minutes

 **Tip:** Top with thin slices of pepperoni, crumbled cooked ground beef or bulk pork sausage, chopped green pepper, canned sliced mushrooms, drained, or grated Parmesan cheese before baking.

# Super Duper Snacks

If the troops need a burst of energy, these simple and tasty snacks will hit the spot!

## Super Easy Pizza Rollers

- **1 package (10 ounces) refrigerated pizza dough**
- **½ cup pizza sauce**
- **18 slices turkey pepperoni**
- **6 sticks mozzarella cheese**

**1.** Preheat oven to 425°F. Coat baking sheet with nonstick cooking spray.

**2.** Roll out pizza dough on baking sheet to form 12×9-inch rectangle. Cut pizza dough into 6 (4½×4-inch) rectangles. Spread about 1 tablespoon sauce over center third of each rectangle. Top with 3 slices pepperoni and stick of mozzarella cheese. Bring ends of dough together over cheese, pinching to seal. Place, seam side down, on prepared baking sheet.

**3.** Bake in center of oven 10 minutes or until golden brown.

*Makes 6 servings*

Little Helpers

Oven temperatures can vary depending on the oven, so watch baking times carefully. Check for doneness using the test given in the recipe.

# Easy Nachos

4 (6-inch) flour tortillas
  Nonstick cooking spray
4 ounces ground turkey
⅔ cup salsa (mild or medium)
2 tablespoons sliced green onion
½ cup (2 ounces) shredded reduced-fat Cheddar cheese

**1.** Preheat oven to 350°F. Cut each tortilla into 8 wedges; lightly spray one side of wedges with cooking spray. Place on ungreased baking sheet. Bake for 5 to 9 minutes or until lightly browned and crisp.

**2.** Cook ground turkey in small nonstick skillet until browned, stirring with spoon to break up meat. Drain fat. Stir in salsa. Cook until hot.

**3.** Sprinkle meat mixture over tortilla wedges. Sprinkle with green onion. Top with cheese. Return to oven 1 to 2 minutes or until cheese melts.

*Makes 4 servings*

# Cheddar Tomato Bacon Toasts

1 jar (16 ounces) RAGÚ® Cheese Creations!® Double Cheddar Sauce
1 medium tomato, chopped
5 slices bacon, crisp-cooked and crumbled (about ⅓ cup)
2 loaves Italian bread (each about 16 inches long), each cut into
    16 slices

**1.** Preheat oven to 350°F. In medium bowl, combine Ragú Cheese Creations! Sauce, tomato and bacon.

**2.** On baking sheet, arrange bread slices. Evenly top with sauce mixture.

**3.** Bake 10 minutes or until sauce mixture is bubbling. Serve immediately.

*Makes 16 servings*

**Prep Time:** 10 minutes
**Cook Time:** 10 minutes

*Easy Nachos*

# Bread Pudding Snacks

1¼ cups reduced-fat (2%) milk
½ cup cholesterol-free egg substitute
⅓ cup sugar
1 teaspoon vanilla
⅛ teaspoon salt
⅛ teaspoon ground nutmeg (optional)
4 cups (½-inch) cinnamon or cinnamon-raisin bread cubes (about 6 bread slices)
1 tablespoon margarine or butter, melted

**1.** Combine milk, egg substitute, sugar, vanilla, salt and nutmeg in medium bowl; mix well. Add bread; mix until well moistened. Let stand at room temperature 15 minutes.

**2.** Preheat oven to 350°F. Line 12 medium-sized muffin cups with paper liners.

**3.** Spoon bread mixture evenly into prepared cups; drizzle evenly with margarine.

**4.** Bake 30 to 35 minutes or until snacks are puffed and golden brown. Remove to wire rack to cool completely. *Makes 12 servings*

---

**Tip**

These snacks will puff up in the oven and fall slightly upon cooling, as many bread puddings tend to do. Be sure to use the type of bread called for in the recipe. Using a different bread can affect the amount of liquid absorbed.

*Bread Pudding Snacks*

# One Potato, Two Potato

**Nonstick cooking spray**
2 **medium baking potatoes, cut lengthwise into 4 wedges**
**Salt**
½ **cup unseasoned dry bread crumbs**
2 **tablespoons grated Parmesan cheese (optional)**
1½ **teaspoons dried oregano leaves, dill weed, Italian herbs or paprika**
**Spicy brown or honey mustard, ketchup or reduced-fat sour cream**

**1.** Preheat oven to 425°F. Spray baking sheet with nonstick cooking spray; set aside.

**2.** Spray cut sides of potatoes generously with cooking spray; sprinkle lightly with salt.

**3.** Combine bread crumbs, Parmesan cheese and desired herb in shallow dish. Add potatoes; toss lightly until potatoes are generously coated with crumb mixture. Place on prepared baking sheet.

**4.** Bake potatoes until browned and tender, about 20 minutes. Serve warm as dippers with mustard. *Makes 4 servings*

**Tip**

If your kids prefer sweet potatoes to regular potatoes, try making Potato Sweets. Omit Parmesan cheese, herbs and mustard. Substitute sweet potatoes for baking potatoes. Cut and spray potatoes as directed; coat generously with desired amount of cinnamon-sugar. Bake as directed. Serve warm as dippers with peach or pineapple preserves or honey mustard.

# Peanut Pitas

 1 package (8 ounces) small pita breads, cut crosswise in half
16 teaspoons reduced-fat peanut butter
16 teaspoons strawberry spreadable fruit
 1 large banana, peeled and thinly sliced (about 48 slices)

**1.** Spread inside of each pita half with 1 teaspoon each peanut butter and spreadable fruit.

**2.** Fill pita halves evenly with banana slices. Serve immediately.

*Makes 8 servings*

**Honey Bees:** Substitute honey for spreadable fruit.

**Jolly Jellies:** Substitute any flavor jelly for spreadable fruit and thin apple slices for banana slices.

**P. B. Crunchers:** Substitute reduced fat mayonnaise for spreadable fruit and celery slices for banana slices.

# Cheesy Barbecued Bean Dip

½ cup canned vegetarian baked beans
3 tablespoons pasteurized process cheese spread
2 tablespoons regular or hickory smoke barbecue sauce
2 large carrots, cut into diagonal slices
1 medium red or green bell pepper, cut into chunks

**1.** Place beans in small microwavable bowl; mash slightly with fork. Stir in process cheese spread and barbecue sauce. Cover with vented plastic wrap.

**2.** Microwave at HIGH 1 minute; stir. Microwave 30 seconds or until hot. Garnish with green onion and bell pepper cutouts, if desired. Serve with carrot and bell pepper dippers.

*Makes 4 servings*

*Peanut Pitas*

# Savory Pita Chips

2  whole wheat or white pita bread rounds
   Olive oil-flavored nonstick cooking spray
3  tablespoons grated Parmesan cheese
1  teaspoon dried basil leaves
¼  teaspoon garlic powder

1. Preheat oven to 350°F. Line baking sheet with foil; set aside.

2. Using small scissors, carefully split each pita bread round around edges; separate to form 2 rounds. Cut each round into 6 wedges.

3. Place wedges, rough side down, on prepared baking sheet; coat lightly with cooking spray. Turn wedges over; spray again.

4. Combine Parmesan cheese, basil and garlic powder in small bowl; sprinkle evenly over pita wedges.

5. Bake 12 to 14 minutes or until golden brown. Cool completely.

*Makes 4 servings*

### Little Helpers

To make a sweet Cinnamon Crisp version, substitute butter-flavored cooking spray for olive oil-flavored spray, and 1 tablespoon sugar mixed with ¼ teaspoon ground cinnamon for Parmesan cheese, basil and garlic powder.

# Cinnamon Trail Mix

- 2 cups corn cereal squares
- 2 cups whole wheat cereal squares or whole wheat cereal squares with mini graham crackers
- 1½ cups fat-free oyster crackers
- ½ cup broken sesame snack sticks
- 2 tablespoons margarine or butter, melted
- 1 teaspoon ground cinnamon
- ¼ teaspoon ground nutmeg
- ½ cup bite-sized fruit-flavored candy pieces

**1.** Preheat oven to 350°F. Spray 13×9-inch baking pan with nonstick cooking spray.

**2.** Place cereals, oyster crackers and sesame sticks in prepared pan; mix lightly.

**3.** Combine margarine, cinnamon and nutmeg in small bowl; mix well. Drizzle evenly over cereal mixture; toss to coat.

**4.** Bake 12 to 14 minutes or until golden brown, stirring gently after 6 minutes. Cool completely. Stir in candies. *Makes 8 (¾-cup) servings*

# Vegetable-Stuffed Baked Potatoes

- 1 jar (16 ounces) RAGÚ® Cheese Creations!® Roasted Garlic Parmesan Sauce or Double Cheddar Sauce
- 1 bag (16 ounces) frozen assorted vegetables, cooked and drained
- 6 large baking potatoes, unpeeled and baked

In 2-quart saucepan, heat Ragú Cheese Creations! Sauce. Stir in vegetables; heat through.

Cut a lengthwise slice from top of each potato. Lightly mash pulp in each potato. Evenly spoon sauce mixture onto each potato. Sprinkle, if desired, with ground black pepper. *Makes 6 servings*

# Delicious Dinners

Gather the whole gang around the dinner table—these special suppers are sure to please.

## Western Wagon Wheels

**1** pound lean ground beef or ground turkey
**2** cups wagon wheel pasta, uncooked
**1** can (14½ ounces) stewed tomatoes
**1½** cups water
**1** box (10 ounces) BIRDS EYE® frozen Sweet Corn
**½** cup barbecue sauce
    **Salt and pepper to taste**

• In large skillet, cook beef over medium heat 5 minutes or until well browned.

• Stir in pasta, tomatoes, water, corn and barbecue sauce; bring to a boil.

• Reduce heat to low; cover and simmer 15 to 20 minutes or until pasta is tender, stirring occasionally. Season with salt and pepper.    *Makes 4 servings*

**Serving Suggestion:** Serve with corn bread or corn muffins.

**Prep Time:** 5 minutes
**Cook Time:** 25 minutes

# Campbell's® Best Ever Meatloaf

1 **can (10¾ ounces) CAMPBELL'S® Condensed Tomato Soup**
2 **pounds ground beef**
1 **pouch CAMPBELL'S® Dry Onion Soup and Recipe Mix**
½ **cup dry bread crumbs**
1 **egg, beaten**
¼ **cup water**

**1.** Mix *½ cup* tomato soup, beef, onion soup mix, bread crumbs and egg *thoroughly*. In baking pan shape *firmly* into 8- by 4-inch loaf.

**2.** Bake at 350°F. for 1¼ hours or until meat loaf is no longer pink (160°F.).

**3.** In small saucepan mix *2 tablespoons* drippings, remaining tomato soup and water. Heat through. Serve with meat loaf.                *Makes 8 servings*

**Prep Time:** 10 minutes
**Cook Time:** 1 hour 20 minutes

**Little Helpers**

All work surfaces, including knives and cutting boards, should be throughly cleaned with hot soapy water after touching raw meat, poultry, seafood or eggs.

# Prego® Miracle Lasagna

1  jar (28 ounces) PREGO® Traditional Pasta Sauce
6  *uncooked* lasagna noodles
1  container (15 ounces) ricotta cheese
8  ounces shredded mozzarella cheese (2 cups)
¼  cup grated Parmesan cheese

**1.** In 2-quart shallow baking dish (11- by 7-inch) spread *1 cup* pasta sauce. Top with *3 uncooked* lasagna noodles, ricotta cheese, *1 cup* mozzarella cheese, Parmesan cheese and *1 cup* pasta sauce. Top with remaining *3 uncooked* lasagna noodles and remaining pasta sauce. **Cover.**

**2.** Bake at 375°F. for 1 hour. Uncover and top with remaining mozzarella cheese. Let stand 5 minutes.                    *Makes 6 servings*

**Meat or Mushroom Miracle Lasagna:** Use 3-quart shallow baking dish (13- by 9-inch). Proceed as in Step 1. Top Parmesan cheese with 1 pound ground beef *or* sausage, cooked and drained, *or* 2 cups sliced fresh mushrooms *or* 2 jars (4½ ounces *each*) sliced mushrooms, drained.

**Prep Time:** 5 minutes
**Cook Time:** 1 hour
**Stand Time:** 5 minutes

 **Tip** For a variation, substitute PREGO® Pasta Sauce with Fresh Mushrooms or PREGO® Italian Sausage & Garlic Pasta Sauce.

# Crunchy Fish Sticks with Rainbow Parmesan Pasta

⅔ cup milk
2 tablespoons margarine or butter
1 (5.1-ounce) package PASTA RONI® Angel Hair Pasta with Parmesan
   Cheese
2 cups frozen mixed vegetables or frozen chopped broccoli
   Crunchy Fish Sticks (recipe follows)

**1.** In large saucepan, bring 1⅓ cups water, milk and margarine to a boil.

**2.** Stir in pasta, vegetables and Special Seasonings; bring back to a boil.
Reduce heat to medium. Gently boil uncovered, 4 to 5 minutes or until pasta
is tender. Let stand 3 minutes before serving. Serve with Crunchy Fish Sticks
or prepared frozen fish sticks. *Makes 4 servings*

**Prep Time:** 20 minutes
**Cook Time:** 15 minutes

## Crunchy Fish Sticks

3 tablespoons all-purpose flour
½ teaspoon ground black pepper
1 large egg
2 tablespoons milk
3 cups cornflakes, coarsely crushed
1 pound cod fillets, cut into 3×1-inch strips and patted dry
½ to ¾ cup vegetable oil

**1.** In shallow bowl, combine flour and pepper; set aside. In small bowl,
combine egg and milk; set aside. In another shallow bowl, place crushed
cornflakes; set aside.

**2.** Coat fish in flour mixture, dip in egg mixture, then roll in cornflakes,
pressing coating gently on each fish strip.

**3.** In large skillet over medium heat, heat oil. Add fish strips; cook 3 to
4 minutes on each side or until golden brown and fish is cooked through.
Drain. *Makes 4 servings*

*Crunchy Fish Sticks with Rainbow Parmesan Pasta*

# Octo-Dogs and Shells

  4  **hot dogs**
1½  **cups uncooked small shell pasta**
1½  **cups frozen mixed vegetables**
  1  **cup prepared Alfredo sauce**
     **Prepared yellow mustard in squeeze bottle**
     **Cheese-flavored fish-shaped crackers**

Lay 1 hot dog on side with end facing you. Starting 1 inch from one end of hot dog, slice hot dog vertically in half. Roll hot dog ¼ turn and slice in half vertically again, making 4 segments connected at the top. Slice each segment in half vertically, creating a total of 8 "legs." Repeat with remaining hot dogs.

Place hot dogs in medium saucepan; cover with water. Bring to a boil over medium-high heat. Remove from heat; set aside.

Prepare pasta according to package directions, stirring in vegetables during last 3 minutes of cooking time. Drain; return to pan. Stir in Alfredo sauce. Heat over low heat until heated through. Divide pasta mixture between four plates.

Drain octo-dogs. Arrange one octo-dog on top of pasta mixture on each plate. Draw faces on "heads" of octo-dogs with mustard. Sprinkle crackers over pasta mixture.

*Makes 4 servings*

# Campbell's® Quick Beef 'n' Beans Tacos

Super Easy

1 **pound ground beef**
1 **small onion, chopped (about ¼ cup)**
1 **can (11¼ ounces) CAMPBELL'S® Condensed Fiesta Chili Beef Soup**
¼ **cup water**
10 **taco shells**
**Shredded Cheddar cheese, shredded lettuce, diced tomato and sour cream**

**1.** In medium skillet over medium-high heat, cook beef and onion until beef is browned, stirring to separate meat. Pour off fat.

**2.** Add soup and water. Reduce heat to low. Cover and cook 5 minutes.

**3.** Divide meat mixture among taco shells. Top with cheese, lettuce, tomato and sour cream.

*Makes 10 tacos*

**Prep Time:** 15 minutes
**Cook Time:** 10 minutes

# Chuckwagon BBQ Rice Round-Up

1 **pound lean ground beef**
1 **(6.8-ounce) package RICE-A-RONI® Beef Flavor**
2 **tablespoons margarine or butter**
2 **cups frozen corn**
½ **cup prepared barbecue sauce**
½ **cup (2 ounces) shredded Cheddar cheese**

**1.** In large skillet over medium-high heat, brown ground beef until well cooked. Remove from skillet; drain. Set aside.

**2.** In same skillet over medium heat, sauté rice-vermicelli mix with margarine until vermicelli is golden brown.

**3.** Slowly stir in 2½ cups water, corn and Special Seasonings; bring to a boil. Reduce heat to low. Cover; simmer 15 to 20 minutes or until rice is tender.

**4.** Stir in barbecue sauce and ground beef. Sprinkle with cheese. Cover; let stand 3 to 5 minutes or until cheese is melted.          *Makes 4 servings*

**Prep Time:** 5 minutes
**Cook Time:** 25 minutes

Salsa can be substituted for barbecue sauce.

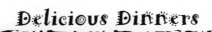
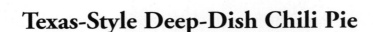

# Texas-Style Deep-Dish Chili Pie

1 tablespoon vegetable oil
1 pound beef stew meat, cut into ½-inch cubes
2 cans (14½ ounces each) Mexican-style stewed tomatoes, undrained
1 medium green bell pepper, diced
1 package (1.0 ounce) LAWRY'S® Taco Spices & Seasonings
1 tablespoon yellow cornmeal
1 can (15¼ ounces) kidney beans, drained
1 package (15 ounces) flat refrigerated pie crusts
½ cup (2 ounces) shredded cheddar cheese, divided

In Dutch oven, heat oil. Cook beef over medium-high heat until browned;
drain fat. Add stewed tomatoes, bell pepper, Taco Spices & Seasonings and
cornmeal. Bring to a boil over medium-high heat; reduce heat to low and cook,
uncovered, 20 minutes. Add kidney beans; mix well. In 10-inch pie plate,
unfold 1 crust and fill with chili mixture and ¼ cup cheese. Top with
remaining crust, fluting edges. Bake, uncovered, in 350°F oven 30 minutes.
Sprinkle remaining cheese over crust; return to oven and bake 10 minutes
longer. *Makes 6 servings*

**Serving Suggestion:** Serve with an orange and red onion salad.

# Turkey Vegetable Chili Mac

Nonstick cooking spray
¾ pound ground turkey breast
½ cup chopped onion
2 cloves garlic, minced
1 can (about 15 ounces) black beans, rinsed and drained
1 can (14½ ounces) Mexican-style stewed tomatoes, undrained
1 can (14½ ounces) no-salt-added diced tomatoes, undrained
1 cup frozen corn
1 teaspoon Mexican seasoning
½ cup uncooked elbow macaroni
⅓ cup reduced-fat sour cream

1. Spray large nonstick saucepan or Dutch oven with cooking spray; heat over medium heat until hot. Add turkey, onion and garlic; cook 5 minutes or until turkey is no longer pink, stirring to crumble.

2. Stir beans, tomatoes with liquid, corn and Mexican seasoning into saucepan; bring to a boil over high heat. Cover; reduce heat to low. Simmer 15 minutes, stirring occasionally.

3. Meanwhile, cook pasta according to package directions, omitting salt. Rinse and drain pasta; stir into saucepan. Simmer, uncovered, 2 to 3 minutes or until heated through.

4. Top each serving with dollop of sour cream. Garnish as desired.

*Makes 6 servings*

*Turkey Vegetable Chili Mac*

# Swinging Sweets

When sweet tooth cravings hit the little ones, be ready with goodies they'll love to eat and share.

 **Super Easy** ## Snackin' Banana Split

1 ripe small banana, peeled
1 small scoop vanilla nonfat or low-fat frozen yogurt (about 3 tablespoons)
1 small scoop strawberry nonfat or low-fat frozen yogurt (about 3 tablespoons)
⅓ cup sliced fresh strawberries or blueberries
2 tablespoons no-sugar-added strawberry fruit spread
1 teaspoon hot water
2 tablespoons low-fat granola cereal
1 maraschino cherry (optional)

**1.** Split banana in half lengthwise. Place in shallow bowl; top with frozen yogurt and strawberries.

**2.** Combine fruit spread and water in small bowl; mix well. Spoon over yogurt; sprinkle with granola. Top with cherry, if desired.

*Makes 1 serving*

# Peanut Butter S'Mores

1½  cups all-purpose flour
 ½  teaspoon baking powder
 ½  teaspoon baking soda
 ¼  teaspoon salt
 ½  cup butter, softened
 ½  cup granulated sugar
 ½  cup packed brown sugar
 ½  cup creamy or chunky peanut butter
  1  egg
  1  teaspoon vanilla
 ½  cup chopped roasted peanuts (optional)
 16  large marshmallows
  4  (1.55-ounce) milk chocolate candy bars

1. Preheat oven to 350°F.

2. Combine flour, baking powder, baking soda and salt in small bowl; set aside. Beat butter, granulated sugar and brown sugar in large bowl of electric mixer at medium speed until light and fluffy. Beat in peanut butter, egg and vanilla until well blended. Gradually beat in flour mixture on low speed until blended. Stir in peanuts, if desired.

3. Roll dough into 1-inch balls; place 2 inches apart on ungreased cookie sheets. Flatten dough with tines of fork, forming criss-cross pattern. Bake about 14 minutes or until set and edges are light golden brown. Cool cookies 2 minutes on cookie sheets; transfer to wire cooling racks. Cool completely.

4. To assemble sandwiches, break each candy bar into four sections. Place 1 section of chocolate on flat side of 1 cookie. Place on microwavable plate; top with 1 marshmallow. Microwave at HIGH 10 to 12 seconds or until marshmallow is puffy. Immediately top with another cookie, flat side down. Press slightly on top cookie, spreading marshmallow to edges. Repeat with remaining cookies one at a time. Cool completely.

*Makes about 16 cookies*

# Bird's Nest Cookies

1⅓ cups (3½ ounces) flaked coconut
1 cup (2 sticks) butter or margarine, softened
½ cup granulated sugar
1 large egg
½ teaspoon vanilla extract
2 cups all-purpose flour
¾ teaspoon salt
1¾ cups "M&M's"® Semi-Sweet Chocolate Mini Baking Bits, divided

Preheat oven to 300°F. Spread coconut on ungreased cookie sheet. Toast in oven, stirring until coconut just begins to turn light golden, about 25 minutes. Remove coconut from cookie sheet; set aside. Increase oven temperature to 350°F. In large bowl cream butter and sugar until light and fluffy; beat in egg and vanilla. In medium bowl combine flour and salt; blend into creamed mixture. Stir in 1 cup "M&M's"® Semi-Sweet Chocolate Mini Baking Bits. Form dough into 1¼-inch balls. Roll heavily in toasted coconut. Place 2 inches apart on lightly greased cookie sheets. Make indentation in center of each cookie with thumb. Bake 12 to 14 minutes or until coconut is golden brown. Remove cookies to wire racks; immediately fill indentations with remaining "M&M's"® Semi-Sweet Chocolate Mini Baking Bits, using scant teaspoonful for each cookie. Cool completely. *Makes about 3 dozen cookies*

## Little Helpers

To grease cookie sheets, use shortening or vegetable cooking spray for the best results. Lining the sheets with parchment paper instead of greasing cuts cleanup and bakes the cookies more evenly.

 # Chocolate Chip Raspberry Jumbles

**1 package DUNCAN HINES® Chocolate Chip Cookie Mix**
**½ cup seedless red raspberry jam**

Preheat oven to 350°F.

Prepare chocolate chip cookie mix as directed on package. Reserve ½ cup dough.

Spread remaining dough into *ungreased* 9-inch square pan. Spread jam over base. Drop reserved dough by measuring teaspoonfuls randomly over jam. Bake 20 to 25 minutes or until golden brown. Cool completely. Cut into bars.

*Makes 16 bars*

 # No-Bake Gingersnap Balls

**20 gingersnap cookies (about 5 ounces)**
**3 tablespoons dark corn syrup**
**2 tablespoons creamy peanut butter**
**⅓ cup powdered sugar**

1. Place cookies in large resealable plastic food storage bag; crush finely with rolling pin or meat mallet.

2. Combine corn syrup and peanut butter in medium bowl. Add crushed gingersnaps; mix well.

3. Roll mixture into 24 (1-inch) balls; coat with powdered sugar.

*Makes 8 servings*

 ## Clown-Around Cones

4 waffle cones
½ cup "M&M's"® Chocolate Mini Baking Bits, divided
  Prepared decorator icing
½ cup hot fudge ice cream topping, divided
4 cups any flavor ice cream, softened
1 (1.5- to 2-ounce) chocolate candy bar, chopped
¼ cup caramel ice cream topping

Decorate cones as desired with "M&M's"® Chocolate Mini Baking Bits, using decorator icing to attach; let set. For each cone, place 1 tablespoon hot fudge topping in bottom of cone. Sprinkle with 1 teaspoon "M&M's"® Chocolate Mini Baking Bits. Layer with 2 tablespoons ice cream; sprinkle with ¼ of candy bar. Layer with ¼ cup ice cream; sprinkle with 1 teaspoon "M&M's"® Chocolate Mini Baking Bits. Top with 1 tablespoon caramel topping and remaining ½ cup ice cream. Wrap in plastic wrap and freeze until ready to serve. Just before serving, top each ice cream cone with 1 tablespoon hot fudge topping; sprinkle with remaining "M&M's"® Chocolate Mini Baking Bits. Serve immediately. *Makes 4 servings*

 ## Ice Cream Pudding Pie

1 cup cold milk
1 cup ice cream (any flavor), softened
1 package (4-serving size) JELL-O® Instant Pudding & Pie Filling, any flavor
1 prepared graham cracker crumb crust (6 ounces)

**MIX** milk and ice cream in large bowl. Add pudding mix. Beat with electric mixer on lowest speed 1 minute. Pour immediately into crust.

**REFRIGERATE** 2 hours or until set. *Makes 8 servings*

Preparation Time: 10 minutes
Refrigerating Time: 2 hours

 **Super Easy**

# Gingerbread Squares

3 tablespoons margarine, softened
2 tablespoons light brown sugar
¼ cup molasses
1 egg white
1¼ cups all-purpose flour
½ teaspoon ground ginger
½ teaspoon ground cinnamon
½ teaspoon baking soda
¼ teaspoon salt
1 cup sweetened applesauce
   Decorations: tube frostings, colored sugars, red hot cinnamon
      candies or other small candies (optional)

1. Preheat oven to 350°F. Spray 8-inch square baking pan with nonstick cooking spray; set aside.

2. Beat margarine and sugar with wooden spoon in medium bowl until well blended. Beat in molasses and egg white.

3. Combine dry ingredients in small bowl; mix well. Add to margarine mixture alternately with applesauce, mixing well after each addition. Transfer batter to prepared pan.

4. Bake 25 to 30 minutes or until wooden pick inserted in center comes out clean. Cool completely on wire rack. Cut into squares. Frost and decorate, if desired.

*Makes 9 servings*

# Peanut Butter Critter Cookies

   **3**  **cups all-purpose flour**
   **1**  **cup peanut butter chips, melted**
  **¾**  **cup granulated sugar**
  **¼**  **cup packed brown sugar**
   **1**  **cup butter, softened**
   **1**  **egg**
  **½**  **tablespoon milk**
   **1**  **teaspoon vanilla**
     **Powdered sugar**
     **Prepared icing**

**1.** Combine flour, melted peanut butter chips, granulated sugar, brown sugar, butter, egg, milk and vanilla in large bowl. Beat at low speed 1 to 2 minutes, scraping bowl often, until well mixed. Divide dough into halves. Wrap in waxed paper; refrigerate until firm, 1 to 2 hours.

**2.** Preheat oven to 375°F. Roll out dough on well-floured surface to ⅛-inch thickness. Cut out desired shapes using 2½-inch cookie cutters. Place 1 inch apart on ungreased cookie sheets. Bake 5 to 8 minutes or until edges are lightly browned. Remove immediately to wire racks, cool completely. Sprinkle with powdered sugar or decorate with icing as desired.

*Makes about 4 dozen cookies*

**Little Helpers**

Chilled cookie dough is easier to handle when making cutouts. Remove only enough dough from the refrigerator to work with at one time. Be sure to save any trimmings; reroll them together to prevent the dough from becoming tough. To minimize sticking of dough when using cookie cutters, dip cutters in flour or spray with vegetable cooking spray.

# Lollipop Sugar Cookies

1¼ **cups granulated sugar**
  1 **Butter Flavor\* CRISCO® Stick or 1 cup Butter Flavor CRISCO®**
     **all-vegetable shortening**
  2 **eggs**
¼ **cup light corn syrup or regular pancake syrup**
  1 **tablespoon vanilla**
  3 **cups all-purpose flour**
¾ **teaspoon baking powder**
½ **teaspoon baking soda**
½ **teaspoon salt**
    **Colored sugars, decorative sprinkles or jimmies**
20 **flat ice cream sticks**

*\*Butter Flavor Crisco is artificially flavored.*

1. Combine sugar and 1 cup shortening in large bowl. Beat at medium speed of electric mixer until well blended. Add eggs, syrup and vanilla. Beat until well blended and fluffy.

2. Combine flour, baking powder, baking soda and salt. Add gradually to creamed mixture at low speed. Mix until well blended. Wrap dough in plastic wrap. Refrigerate at least 1 hour. Keep refrigerated until ready to use.

3. Heat oven to 375°F. Place sheets of foil on countertop for cooling cookies.

4. Place sprinkles, jimmies or colored sugar in shallow bowl. Shape dough into 2-inch balls. Roll ball in sprinkles, jimmies or colored sugar. Insert ice cream stick into each dough ball. Place dough balls with sticks 3 inches apart on ungreased baking sheets. Flatten dough balls slightly with spatula.

5. Bake one baking sheet at a time at 375°F for 7 to 9 minutes or until barely browned. *Do not overbake.* Cool 2 minutes on baking sheets. Remove cookies to foil to cool completely.                *Makes about 20 cookies*

# Poppin' Party Treats

Cakes, cookies, munchies and more—these are sure to make your kids' parties exciting and memorable.

## Picnic Pizza Biscuits

**1** can (10 ounces) refrigerated buttermilk biscuits
**1** pound hot Italian sausage, casings removed
**½** cup chopped onion
**½** cup sliced mushrooms
**½** cup chopped green bell pepper
**½** cup (2 ounces) shredded mozzarella cheese
**¼** cup marinara or pizza sauce
**2** tablespoons *French's*® Dijon Mustard

**1.** Preheat oven to 375°F. Separate biscuits; pat or roll into 10 (4-inch) circles on floured surface. Press circles into 12-cup muffin pan.

**2.** Cook sausage in large nonstick skillet over high heat 5 minutes or until browned, stirring to separate meat; drain fat. Add onion, mushrooms and bell pepper; cook and stir 3 minutes or until vegetables are tender. Stir in cheese, sauce and mustard; mix well.

**3.** Mound filling evenly in biscuits. Bake 20 minutes or until biscuits are browned. Serve warm or at room temperature. *Makes 10 servings*

**Prep Time:** 30 minutes
**Cook Time:** 25 minutes

# Rock 'n' Rollers

4 (6- to 7-inch) flour tortillas
4 ounces Neufchâtel cheese, softened
⅓ cup peach preserves
1 cup (4 ounces) shredded nonfat Cheddar cheese
½ cup packed washed fresh spinach leaves
3 ounces thinly sliced regular or smoked turkey breast

**1.** Spread each tortilla evenly with 1 ounce Neufchâtel cheese; cover with thin layer of preserves. Sprinkle with Cheddar cheese.

**2.** Arrange spinach leaves and turkey over Cheddar cheese. Roll up tortillas; trim ends. Cover and refrigerate until ready to serve.

**3.** Cut "rollers" crosswise in half or diagonally into 1-inch pieces.

*Makes 8 servings*

**Sassy Salsa Rollers:** Substitute salsa for peach preserves and shredded iceberg lettuce for spinach leaves.

**Ham 'n' Apple Rollers:** Omit peach preserves and spinach leaves. Substitute lean ham slices for turkey. Spread tortillas with Neufchâtel cheese as directed; sprinkle with Cheddar cheese. Top each tortilla with about 2 tablespoons finely chopped apple and 2 ham slices; roll up. Continue as directed.

**Wedgies:** Prepare Rock 'n' Rollers or any variation as directed, but do not roll up. Top with a second tortilla; cut into wedges.

A tortilla is a thin, flat bread made from wheat or corn flour. They are baked on a griddle or heavy frying pan and can be served in a variety of ways.

# Hot Dog Cookies

**1 recipe Butter Cookie Dough (recipe page 72)**
**Liquid food colors**
**Sesame seeds**
**Shredded coconut, red and green decorator gels, frosting and**
**gummy candies**

**1.** Prepare Butter Cookie Dough. Cover; refrigerate 4 hours or until firm. Grease cookie sheets.

**2.** Use ⅓ of dough to make "hot dogs." Refrigerate remaining dough. Mix food colors in small bowl to get reddish-brown color following chart on back of food color box. Add reserved ⅓ of dough. Mix color throughout dough using wooden spoon.

**3.** Divide colored dough into 6 equal sections. Roll each section into thin log shape. Round edges. Set aside.

**4.** To make "buns," divide remaining dough into 6 equal sections. Roll sections into thick logs. Make very deep indentation the length of log in centers; smooth edges to create buns. Lift buns with small spatula and dip sides in sesame seeds. Place 3 inches apart on prepared cookie sheets. Place hot dogs inside buns. Freeze 20 minutes.

**5.** Preheat oven to 350°F. Bake 17 to 20 minutes or until bun edges are light golden brown. Cool completely on cookie sheets.

**6.** Top hot dogs with green-tinted shredded coconut for "relish," white coconut for "onions," red decorator gel for "ketchup" and yellow-tinted frosting or whipped topping for "mustard."           *Makes 6 hot dog cookies*

**Tip**

To pipe gels and frosting onto Hot Dog Cookies, you can use a resealable plastic sandwich bag as a substitute for a pastry bag. Fold the top of the bag down to form a cuff and use a spatula to fill bag half full with gel or frosting. Unfold top of bag and twist down against the filling. Snip a tiny tip off one corner of bag. Hold top of bag tightly and squeeze the filling through the opening.

**continued on page 72**

*Hot Dog Cookies*

**Hot Dog Cookies, continued**

### Butter Cookie Dough

¾ **cup butter, softened**
¼ **cup granulated sugar**
¼ **cup packed light brown sugar**
1 **egg yolk**
1¾ **cups all-purpose flour**
¾ **teaspoon baking powder**
⅛ **teaspoon salt**

**1.** Combine butter, granulated sugar, brown sugar and egg yolk in medium bowl. Add flour, baking powder and salt; mix well.

**2.** Cover; refrigerate about 4 hours or until firm.

 ### Tic-Tac-Toe Pie

**Vanilla wafer cookies**
1½ **cups cold milk**
1 **package (4-serving size) JELL-O® Vanilla Flavor Instant Pudding and Pie Filling**
1 **tub (8 ounces) COOL WHIP® Whipped Topping, thawed**
**Assorted miniature cookies**

**LINE** bottom and sides of 9-inch pie plate with vanilla wafer cookies.

**POUR** milk into large bowl. Add pudding mix. Beat with wire whisk 1 to 2 minutes. Let stand 5 minutes or until slightly thickened. Gently stir in 3 cups of the whipped topping. Spoon into crust.

**FREEZE** 4 hours or overnight until firm. Let stand at room temperature 15 minutes or until pie can be cut easily. Garnish with remaining whipped topping to form lines. Decorate with miniature cookies between the lines to resemble a tic-tac-toe game. Store leftover pie in freezer.

*Makes 8 servings*

# Peanut Butter and Jelly Sandwich Cookies

**1 package (18 ounces) refrigerated sugar cookie dough**
**1 tablespoon unsweetened cocoa powder**
**All-purpose flour (optional)**
**¾ cup creamy peanut butter**
**½ cup grape jam or jelly**

**1.** Remove dough from wrapper according to package directions. Reserve ¼ section of dough; cover and refrigerate remaining ¾ section of dough. Combine reserved dough and cocoa in small bowl; cover and refrigerate.

**2.** Shape remaining ¾ section of dough into 5½-inch log. Sprinkle with flour to minimize sticking, if necessary. Remove chocolate dough from refrigerator; roll on sheet of waxed paper to 9½×6½-inch rectangle. Place dough log in center of rectangle.

**3.** Bring waxed paper edges and chocolate dough up and together over log. Press gently on top and sides of dough so entire log is wrapped in chocolate dough. Flatten log slightly to form square. Wrap in waxed paper. Freeze 10 minutes.

**4.** Preheat oven to 350°F. Remove waxed paper. Cut dough into ¼-inch slices. Place slices 2 inches apart on ungreased cookie sheets. Reshape dough edges into square, if necessary. Press dough slightly to form indentation so dough resembles slice of bread.

**5.** Bake 8 to 11 minutes or until lightly browned. Remove from oven and straighten cookie edges with spatula. Cool 2 minutes on cookie sheets. Remove to wire racks; cool completely.

**6.** To make sandwich, spread about 1 tablespoon peanut butter on bottom of 1 cookie. Spread about ½ tablespoon jam over peanut butter; top with second cookie, pressing gently. Repeat with remaining cookies.

*Makes 11 sandwich cookies*

**Little Helpers**

Cut each sandwich diagonally in half for a smaller cookie and fun look.

# Treasure Chest

1 package (12 ounces) pound cake
1 tub (8 ounces) COOL WHIP® Whipped Topping, thawed
   Assorted "jewels," such as: fruit chews, candy necklaces, cubed
      prepared JELL-O® Brand Gelatin, raspberries, gumdrops or other
      small candies
1 pretzel rod, cut into 3 pieces
   Miniature candy-coated semi-sweet chocolate candies
   Black licorice
2 pretzels

**CUT** ½-inch-horizontal slice off top of cake; set slice aside. Carefully hollow out center of cake, leaving ½-inch shell on bottom and sides; reserve removed cake for snacking or other use. Spoon 1 cup of the whipped topping into cake shell. Frost sides with 1½ cups whipped topping.

**REFRIGERATE** until ready to serve. Just before serving, place assorted "jewels" over whipped topping in cake shell. Angle reserved cake slice over jewels using pretzel rod pieces to resemble an open chest lid. Frost slice with remaining whipped topping. Decorate with miniature candy-coated semi-sweet chocolate candies and licorice. Add remaining pretzels to ends of chest for handles.
*Makes 8 servings*

## Flag Dessert

- **2 pints fresh strawberries**
- **1 package (12 ounces) pound cake, cut into 16 slices**
- **1⅓ cups blueberries**
- **1 tub (12 ounces) COOL WHIP® Whipped Topping, thawed**

SLICE 1 cup of the strawberries; set aside. Halve remaining strawberries; set aside.

LINE bottom of 12×8-inch glass baking dish with 8 cake slices. Top with 1 cup sliced strawberries, 1 cup of the blueberries and ½ of the whipped topping. Place remaining cake slices over whipped topping. Spread remaining whipped topping over cake. Arrange strawberry halves and remaining ⅓ cup blueberries over whipped topping to create a flag design.

REFRIGERATE until ready to serve. *Makes 15 servings*

## Peppermint Ice Cream Pie

- **4 cups no-sugar-added vanilla ice cream**
- **6 sugar-free peppermint candies**
- **1 reduced-fat graham cracker pie crust**
- **¼ cup sugar-free chocolate syrup**

**1.** Scoop ice cream into medium bowl; let stand at room temperature 5 minutes or until softened, stirring occasionally.

**2.** Place candies in heavy-duty plastic food storage bag; coarsely crush with a rolling pin or meat mallet. Stir candy into ice cream; spread evenly into pie crust.

**3.** Cover; freeze at least 4 hours or overnight. Using sharp knife that has been dipped into warm water, cut pie into slices. Transfer to serving plates; drizzle with chocolate. *Makes 12 servings*

# Radio Fun

**CAKE & FROSTINGS**
1 (9-inch) square cake
1 cup Base Frosting (recipe page 80), if desired
3 cups Buttercream Frosting (recipe page 80)*

**DECORATIONS & EQUIPMENT**
Pink and black licorice pieces
2 yellow candy discs
1 orange flat gumdrop
1 (19×13-inch) cake board, cut into 10×10-inch square and covered
Icing comb
Pastry bags, small writing tip and basketweave tip

*Color 2 cups frosting green and 1 cup yellow.*

**1.** Trim top and edges of cake. Cut as shown in photo. Place cake on prepared cake board. Frost entire cake with Base Frosting to seal in crumbs.

**2.** Frost as shown in photo, reserving small portion of each color for piping. While frosting is soft, use icing comb to make design for speaker.**

**3.** Using flat side of basketweave tip and reserved yellow frosting, pipe two vertical lines, one at end of speaker section and another 2 inches from the first line.

**4.** Using writing tip and reserved green frosting, pipe accents on handle as shown.

**5.** Position candies as shown.                    *Makes 10 to 14 servings*

**Design on speaker can also be made with fork.*

---

**Tip**

An icing or cake comb is a triangular tool with saw-tooth edges used to create different width lines in cake frosting for decorative effect.

---

**continued on page 80**

*Radio Fun*

**Radio Fun, continued**

## Base Frosting

  3  **cups powdered sugar, sifted**
  ½  **cup butter or margarine, softened**
  ¼  **cup milk**
  ½  **teaspoon vanilla**

Combine powdered sugar, butter, milk and vanilla in large bowl. Beat with electric mixer until smooth. Add more milk, 1 teaspoon at a time. Frosting should be fairly thin. *Makes about 2 cups*

## Buttercream Frosting

  6  **cups powdered sugar, sifted and divided**
  ¾  **cup butter or margarine, softened**
  ¼  **cup shortening**
  6  **to 8 tablespoons milk, divided**
  1  **teaspoon vanilla**

Combine 3 cups powdered sugar, butter, shortening, 4 tablespoons milk and vanilla in large bowl. Beat with electric mixer until smooth. Add remaining powdered sugar; beat until light and fluffy, adding more milk, 1 tablespoon at a time, as needed for good spreading consistency. *Makes about 3½ cups*

# Fun Food for Kids

Lots of Great Recipes Inside

# Fun Food for Kids

# Starters & Snacks

## Golden Chicken Nuggets

● **Prep Time:** 5 minutes    ● **Cook Time:** 15 minutes

**1 pound boneless skinless chicken breasts, cut into 1½-inch pieces**
**¼ cup *French's®* Honey Mustard**
**2 cups *French's® Taste Toppers*™ French Fried Onions, finely crushed**

**1.** Preheat oven to 400°F. Toss chicken with mustard in medium bowl.

**2.** Place **Taste Toppers** in resealable plastic food storage bag. Toss chicken in onions, a few pieces at a time, pressing gently to adhere.

**3.** Place nuggets in shallow baking pan. Bake 15 minutes or until chicken is no longer pink in center. Serve with additional honey mustard.

*Makes 4 servings*

Golden Chicken Nuggets

# Kids' Quesadillas

●**Prep Time:** 5 minutes ●**Cook Time:** 15 minutes

8 slices American cheese
8 (10-inch) flour tortillas
½ pound thinly sliced deli turkey
6 tablespoons *French's®* Honey Mustard, divided
2 tablespoons melted butter
¼ teaspoon paprika

**1.** To prepare 1 quesadilla, arrange 2 slices of cheese on 1 tortilla. Top with one-fourth of the turkey. Spread with *1½ tablespoons* mustard, then top with another tortilla. Prepare 3 more quesadillas with remaining ingredients.

**2.** Combine butter and paprika. Brush one side of tortilla with butter mixture. Preheat 12-inch nonstick skillet over medium-high heat. Arrange tortilla butter side down and cook 2 minutes. Brush tortilla with butter mixture and turn over. Cook 1½ minutes or until golden brown. Repeat with remaining three quesadillas. Slice into wedges before serving.                    *Makes 4 servings*

> Add some green or red bell pepper strips to these yummy quesadillas for crunch and an added flavor boost.

**Harry Hound** (page 160)

Kids' Quesadillas

# Teddy Bear Party Mix

● **Prep Time:** 5 minutes  ● **Cook Time:** 12 minutes

- 4 cups crisp cinnamon graham cereal
- 2 cups honey flavored teddy-shaped graham snacks
- 1 can (1½ ounces) *French's*® Potato Sticks
- 3 tablespoons butter, melted
- 2 tablespoons *French's*® Worcestershire Sauce
- 1 tablespoon packed brown sugar
- ¼ teaspoon ground cinnamon
- 1 cup sweetened dried cranberries or raisins
- ½ cup chocolate, peanut butter or carob chips

**1.** Preheat oven to 350°F. Lightly spray jelly-roll pan with nonstick cooking spray. Combine cereal, graham snacks and potato sticks in large bowl.

**2.** Combine butter, Worcestershire, sugar and cinnamon in small bowl; toss with cereal mixture. Transfer to prepared pan. Bake 12 minutes. Cool completely.

**3.** Stir in dried cranberries and chips. Store in an air-tight container.

*Makes about 7 cups*

**Tips to Stay Safe**

**Stop! Don't begin preparing food until you wash your hands with hot soapy water.**

Teddy Bear Party Mix

# Picnic Pizza Muffins

● **Prep Time:** 15 minutes     ● **Cook Time:** 25 minutes

     1 package (about 1 pound) refrigerated grand-size flaky
         buttermilk biscuits
     ½ pound ground beef
     ½ cup chopped green bell pepper
     ½ cup canned sliced mushrooms, drained
     ½ cup prepared pizza sauce
     ½ cup shredded mozzarella cheese
     2 tablespoons *Frank's® RedHot®* Sauce

**1.** Preheat oven to 375°F. Separate biscuits; pat into 3-inch circles. Press circles into muffin cups. Fill empty muffin cups halfway with water; set aside.

**2.** Cook beef and vegetables in large nonstick skillet over high heat 5 to 8 minutes or until meat is browned, stirring to separate meat. Drain fat. Stir in pizza sauce, cheese and *RedHot* Sauce; mix well.

**3.** Mound filling into muffin cups, dividing evenly. Bake 20 minutes or until muffins are browned. Serve warm or at room temperature.

*Makes 8 servings*

**Tip:** For an extra kick of flavor, substitute ground sweet Italian sausage for the ground beef.

# Painted Bread Knots

● **Prep Time:** 10 minutes  ● **Cook Time:** 20 minutes

**1 tablespoon** *French's® Classic Yellow®* **Mustard**

**1 tablespoon milk**

**1 package (11 ounces) refrigerated crusty French loaf dough**
  **Toppings:** *French's® Taste Toppers*™ **French Fried Onions,**
  **crushed, poppy seeds, sesame seeds or coarse salt**

**1.** Preheat oven to 350°F. Combine mustard and milk in small bowl. Cut bread dough into 12 (1-inch) slices. Roll each slice into 8-inch long piece. Tie each into knot.

**2.** Arrange knots on lightly greased baking sheet. Paint each with mustard mixture. Sprinkle with desired toppings. Bake 20 minutes or until golden. Place baking sheet on wire rack and let knots stand on baking sheet until completely cool.

**3.** Serve with additional mustard.          *Makes 12 servings*

**Pierre Pretzel (page 157)**

This is a great recipe to keep kids busy while mom or dad makes dinner.

# Bite Size Tacos

**Prep Time:** 5 minutes ● **Cook Time:** 15 minutes

     1 **pound ground beef**
     1 **package (1.25 ounces) taco seasoning mix**
     2 **cups** *French's® Taste Toppers™* **French Fried Onions**
    ¼ **cup chopped fresh cilantro**
    32 **bite-size round tortilla chips**
    ¾ **cup sour cream**
     1 **cup shredded Cheddar cheese**
       **Frank's® RedHot® Sauce (optional)**

*1.* Cook beef in nonstick skillet over medium-high heat 5 minutes or until browned; drain. Stir in taco seasoning mix, *¾ cup water, 1 cup* **Taste Toppers** and cilantro. Simmer 5 minutes or until flavors are blended, stirring often.

*2.* Preheat oven to 350°F. Arrange tortilla chips on foil-lined baking sheet. Top with beef mixture, sour cream, remaining **Taste Toppers** and cheese.

*3.* Bake 5 minutes or until cheese is melted and **Taste Toppers** are golden. Sprinkle with chopped red bell pepper, if desired. Splash on **RedHot** Sauce to taste.          *Makes 8 appetizer servings*

Bite Size Tacos

# Zesty Fun Pretzel Dip

●**Prep Time:** 5 minutes

½ cup *French's®* Hearty Deli Brown Mustard
½ cup honey

**1.** Combine mustard and honey in small bowl.

**2.** Use for dipping pretzels, chips or cheese cubes.

*Makes 1 cup*


# Cheesy Mustard Dip

●**Prep Time:** 15 minutes

1 container (8 ounces) whipped cream cheese
¼ cup milk
3 tablespoons *French's®* Hearty Deli Brown or Honey
    Mustard
2 tablespoons mayonnaise
2 tablespoons minced green onions

**1.** Combine ingredients in medium bowl; mix until well blended.

*Makes 8 servings (about 1¼ cups dip)*

**Tips to Stay Safe**

Always be prepared. It is important to read the entire recipe and gather all the ingredients and utensils you need before beginning.

Clockwise from left: Cheesy Mustard Dip; Zesty Fun Pretzel Dip; French's® Honey Mustard

# Buffalo Chicken Wings with a Twist

**Prep Time:** 5 minutes    **Cook Time:** 12 minutes

   2½ **pounds chicken wing pieces**
   ½ **cup** *Frank's® RedHot® Sauce*
   ⅓ **cup melted butter**

**1.** Deep-fry\* wings in hot oil (400°F) 12 minutes or until fully cooked and crispy; drain.

**2.** Combine **RedHot** Sauce and butter. Dip wings in sauce to coat.

**3.** Serve wings with celery and blue cheese dressing, if desired.

*Makes 8 appetizer servings*

\*For equally crispy wings, bake wings 1 hour in preheated oven at 425°F, or grill 30 minutes over medium heat.

**Variations:** Add one of the following to **RedHot** butter mixture; heat through:

Sweet 'n' Spicy: ¼ cup orange juice concentrate and ¾ teaspoon ground cinnamon

Tex-Mex: 1 tablespoon chili powder and ¼ teaspoon garlic powder

Asian: 2 tablespoons teriyaki sauce and 2 teaspoons ground ginger

# Festive Nachos

●**Prep Time:** 5 minutes　　●**Cook Time:** 2 minutes

　½ **(10-ounce) package tortilla chips**
　**3 cups Mexican blend shredded cheese**
　**2 cups *French's® Taste Toppers*™ French Fried Onions**
　**1 cup chopped plum tomatoes**
　½ **cup sliced black olives**

**1.** Layer chips, cheese, **Taste Toppers**, tomatoes and olives on microwave-safe plate. Microwave on HIGH 2 to 3 minutes or until cheese melts.

**2.** Serve with salsa and prepared guacamole, if desired.

*Makes 4 servings*


# Saucy Mini Franks

●**Prep Time:** 5 minutes　　●**Cook Time:** 5 minutes

　½ **cup *French's®* Honey Mustard**
　½ **cup chili sauce *or* ketchup**
　½ **cup grape jelly**
　**1 tablespoon *Frank's® RedHot®* Sauce**
　**1 pound mini cocktail franks or 1 pound cooked meatballs**

**1.** Combine mustard, chili sauce, grape jelly and **RedHot** Sauce in saucepan.

**2.** Add cocktail franks. Simmer and stir 5 minutes or until jelly is melted and franks are hot.

*Makes about 6 servings*

# Make Your Own Pizza Shapes

● **Prep Time:** 10 minutes   ● **Cook Time:** 15 minutes

1 package (10 ounces) refrigerated pizza dough
¼ to ½ cup prepared pizza sauce
1 cup shredded mozzarella cheese
1 cup *French's® Taste Toppers™* French Fried Onions
*Frank's® RedHot®* Sauce (optional)

**1.** Preheat oven to 425°F. Unroll dough onto greased baking sheet. Press or roll dough into 12×8-inch rectangle. With sharp knife or large cookie cutter, cut dough into shape of your choice (fish, heart, star). Reroll scraps and cut into mini shapes.

**2.** Pre-bake crust 7 minutes or until crust just begins to brown. Spread with sauce and top with cheese. Bake 6 minutes or until crust is deep golden brown.

**3.** Sprinkle with **Taste Toppers**. Bake 2 minutes longer or until golden. Splash on **RedHot** Sauce to taste.

*Makes 4 to 6 servings*

**Tish the Fish (page 157)**

For extra flavor, sprinkle chopped olives or peppers on the pizza shapes when you add the cheese.

Make Your Own Pizza Shapes

# Spanish Omelet

8 large eggs, beaten
3 cups (16 ounces) frozen cubed or shredded hash brown
    potatoes
1½ cups *French's® Taste Toppers™* French Fried Onions
Salsa
*Frank's® RedHot®* Sauce

**1.** Beat eggs with *½ teaspoon salt* and *¼ teaspoon pepper* in large bowl; set aside.

**2.** Heat *2 tablespoons oil* until very hot in 10-inch nonstick oven-safe skillet over medium-high heat. Sauté potatoes about 7 minutes or until browned, stirring often.

**3.** Stir *½ cup* **Taste Toppers** and beaten eggs into potato mixture. Cook, uncovered, over low heat 15 minutes or until eggs are almost set. *Do not stir.* Sprinkle eggs with remaining *1 cup* **Taste Toppers**. Cover and cook 8 minutes or until eggs are fully set. Cut into wedges and serve with salsa. Splash on **RedHot** Sauce to taste.

*Makes 6 servings*

**Tips to Stay Safe**

Be sure to wrap the handle of the skillet with foil to make it oven-safe. And remember, always use pot holders when handling hot skillets.

Spanish Omelet

# Buffalo-Style Chicken Pizza

●●●●●●●●●●●●●●●●●●●●●●●●●●●●●●●●●●●●●●●●●●●●●●●●●●

●**Prep Time:** 10 minutes   ●**Cook Time:** 15 minutes

  2 **cups diced cooked chicken**
⅓ **cup** *Frank's® RedHot®* **Sauce**
  2 **tablespoons melted butter**
  2 **(12-inch) prebaked pizza shells**
  1 **cup pizza** *or* **barbecue sauce**
  2 **cups shredded mozzarella cheese**
½ **cup diced celery**
½ **cup blue cheese or ranch dressing**

**1.** Preheat oven to 400°F. Toss chicken with **RedHot** Sauce and butter in large bowl.

**2.** Place pizza shells on baking sheets. Spread shells with pizza sauce. Sprinkle with chicken mixture, cheese and celery.

**3.** Bake 15 minutes. Drizzle with dressing. Cut into wedges to serve.     *Makes 8 servings*

# Inside-Out Egg Salad

●●●●●●●●●●●●●●●●●●●●●●●●●●●●●●●●●●●●●●●●●●●●●●●●●●

●**Prep Time:** 20 minutes

  6 **hard-cooked eggs, peeled**
⅓ **cup mayonnaise**
¼ **cup chopped celery**
  1 **tablespoon** *French's® Classic Yellow®* **Mustard**

**1.** Cut eggs in half lengthwise. Remove egg yolks. Combine yolks, mayonnaise, celery and mustard in medium bowl. Add salt and pepper to taste.

**2.** Spoon egg yolk mixture into egg whites. Sprinkle with paprika, if desired. Chill before serving.     *Makes 12 servings*

# French Onion Bread Stix

● **Prep Time:** 5 minutes ● **Cook Time:** 15 minutes

1⅓ cups *French's® Taste Toppers™* French Fried Onions,
    crushed
¼ cup grated Parmesan cheese
 1 package (11 ounces) refrigerated soft bread sticks
 1 egg white, beaten

**1.** Preheat oven to 350°F. Combine **Taste Toppers** and cheese in pie plate. Separate dough into 12 pieces on sheet of waxed paper.

**2.** Brush one side of dough with egg white. Dip pieces wet side down into crumbs, pressing firmly. Baste top surface with egg white and dip into crumbs.

**3.** Twist pieces to form a spiral. Arrange on ungreased baking sheet. Bake 15 to 20 minutes or until golden brown.

*Makes 12 bread sticks*

# Creamy Dip & Spread

● **Prep Time:** 5 minutes

½ cup *French's®* Mustard (any flavor)
½ cup mayonnaise

**1.** Combine all ingredients in small bowl.

*Makes 1 cup*

# Soups & Sandwiches

## Pizza Soup

**Prep Time:** 5 minutes      **Cook Time:** 10 minutes

- **2 cans (10¾ ounces each) condensed tomato soup**
- **¾ teaspoon garlic powder**
- **½ teaspoon dried oregano leaves**
- **¾ cup uncooked tiny pasta shells (¼-inch)**
- **1 cup shredded quick melting mozzarella cheese**
- **1 cup *French's® Taste Toppers*™ French Fried Onions**

**1.** Combine soup, *2 soup cans of water*, garlic powder and oregano in small saucepan. Bring to boiling over medium-high heat.

**2.** Add pasta. Cook 8 minutes or until pasta is tender.

**3.** Stir in cheese. Cook until cheese melts. Sprinkle with **Taste Toppers**.

*Makes 4 servings*

Pizza Soup and French Onion Bread Stix (page 101)

# Mini Mexican Burger Bites

● **Prep Time:** 5 minutes    ● **Cook Time:** 8 minutes

1½ **pounds ground beef**
½ **cup finely chopped red, yellow or green bell pepper**
2 **tablespoons** *French's®* **Worcestershire Sauce**
1 **teaspoon** *Frank's® RedHot®* **Sauce**
1 **teaspoon dried oregano leaves**
¼ **teaspoon salt**
12 **mini dinner rolls**
   **Shredded Cheddar cheese**

**1.** Gently combine all ingredients except rolls and cheese in large bowl. Shape into 12 mini patties. Broil or grill patties 4 to 6 minutes for medium doneness (160°F internal temperature), turning once.

**2.** Arrange lettuce on rolls, if desired. Place burgers on rolls and top with Cheddar cheese.                    *Makes 6 servings*

Make one night a week fiesta night! Serve these yummy burger bites with chips and salsa for a fun family party.

**School Bus** (page 159)

Mini Mexican Burger Bites

# Caribbean Quesadillas

● **Prep Time:** 10 minutes ● **Cook Time:** about 10 minutes

      1 cup cut-up cooked chicken
      1 tablespoon *Frank's® RedHot®* Sauce
      1 tablespoon lime juice
    ¼ cup *French's®* Honey Mustard
      1 cup shredded cheese
      8 (6-inch) flour tortillas

**1.** Toss together chicken, **RedHot** Sauce and lime juice in medium bowl.

**2.** Spread each tortilla with *1 tablespoon* mustard. Sprinkle tortillas with cheese and top with chicken mixture, dividing evenly. Cover each with another tortilla, presssing down firmly to form quesadilla.

**3.** Coat large nonstick skillet with vegetable cooking spray. Cook quesadillas over medium heat about 2 to 3 minutes or until golden, turning once. Cut into wedges to serve.          *Makes 4 servings*


# Chicken Tortilla Soup

● **Prep Time:** 5 minutes ● **Cook Time:** 6 minutes

      1 teaspoon minced garlic
    2½ cups chicken broth
      1 jar (16 ounces) mild chunky-style salsa
      2 cups cooked finely cut-up chicken
      1 cup frozen whole kernel corn
      1 to 2 tablespoons *Frank's® RedHot®* Sauce or more to taste
      1 tablespoon chopped fresh cilantro (optional)
      1 cup crushed tortilla chips

**1.** Heat *1 tablespoon oil* in large saucepan over medium-high heat. Sauté garlic 1 minute or until tender. Add remaining ingredients *except* tortilla chips. Cover; reduce heat to medium-low and simmer 5 minutes.

**2.** Stir in tortilla chips. Sprinkle with shredded Monterey Jack cheese, if desired. Serve while hot.          *Makes 4 to 6 servings*

# Hearty Beef Stew

●**Prep Time:** 5 minutes ●**Cook Time:** 15 minutes

- **1 pound ground beef**
- **1 tablespoon minced garlic**
- **1 jar (14 ounces) marinara sauce**
- **1 can (10½ ounces) condensed beef broth**
- **1 package (16 ounces) Italian-style frozen vegetables**
- **2 cups Southern-style hash brown potatoes**
- **2 tablespoons *French's*® Worcestershire Sauce**
- **2 cups *French's*® *Taste Toppers*™ French Fried Onions**

**1.** Cook beef and garlic in nonstick skillet 5 minutes or until browned. Stir in sauce, broth, vegetables, potatoes and Worcestershire. Bring to boiling; cover. Reduce heat to medium-low. Cook 10 minutes or until vegetables are crisp-tender.

**2.** Spoon soup into bowls. Sprinkle with ***Taste Toppers***. Serve with garlic bread, if desired.

*Makes 6 servings*

**Nosey Nick (page 158)**

Toast ***Taste Toppers*** in the microwave for 1 minute on **HIGH** for extra crispness.

# Grilled Cheese & Turkey Shapes

● **Prep Time:** 15 minutes ● **Cook Time:** 2 minutes

- 8 **slices seedless rye or sourdough bread**
- 8 **teaspoons** *French's*® **Mustard, any flavor**
- 8 **slices deli roast turkey**
- 4 **slices American cheese**
- 2 **tablespoons butter or margarine, softened**

**1.** Spread *1 teaspoon* mustard on each slice of bread. Arrange turkey and cheese on half of the bread slices, dividing evenly. Cover with top halves of bread.

**2.** Cut out sandwich shapes using desired cookie cutters. Place cookie cutter on top of sandwich; press down firmly. Remove excess trimmings.

**3.** Spread butter on both sides of bread. Heat large nonstick skillet over medium heat. Cook sandwiches 1 minute per side or until bread is golden and cheese melts. Decorate with mustard.

*Makes 4 sandwiches*

**Tip:** For extra fun, use 2½-inch teddy bear, cat, star, heart or flower-shaped cookie cutters.

Grilled Cheese & Turkey Shapes

# Chunky Potato Bacon Soup

● **Prep Time:** 5 minutes    ● **Cook Time:** 10 minutes

1 package (32 ounces) frozen Southern-style hash brown
   potatoes, thawed
1 quart milk
1 can (10¾ ounces) condensed cream of celery soup
1 cup (6 ounces) cubed processed cheese
⅓ cup cooked chopped bacon (4 slices uncooked)
1 tablespoon *French's®* Worcestershire Sauce
1⅓ cups *French's® Taste Toppers™* French Fried Onions

**1.** Combine potatoes, milk, soup, cheese, bacon and
Worcestershire in large saucepot. Heat to boiling over medium-high
heat, stirring often.

**2.** Heat **Taste Toppers** in microwave on HIGH 1 minute or until
golden. Ladle soup into bowls. Sprinkle with **Taste Toppers**. Garnish
with fresh minced parsley, if desired.             *Makes 6 servings*

## Tips to Stay Safe

To avoid harmful bacterial growth, don't let hot
food sit on the counter. Be sure to divide any
leftovers into smaller containers and refrigerate right away.

Chunky Potato Bacon Soup and Painted Bread Knots (page 89)

# Tex-Mex Cheddar Cheese Soup

● **Prep Time:** 5 minutes  ● **Cook Time:** 10 minutes

- **2 cans (10¾ ounces each) condensed Cheddar cheese or cream of chicken soup**
- **2 cups milk**
- **1 cup half and half**
- **2 cups shredded Cheddar cheese**
- **1 can (4 ounces) green chilies, finely chopped**
- **1 teaspoon ground cumin**
- **2 cups *French's®* *Taste Toppers*™ French Fried Onions**

**1.** Combine soup, milk and half and half in large saucepan. Heat over medium-high heat until hot. Stir in cheese, chilies and cumin. Cook until cheese melts, stirring constantly.

**2.** Place **Taste Toppers** in microwave-safe dish. Microwave on HIGH 1 minute or until golden.

**3.** Spoon soup into bowls. Garnish with sour cream and fresh cilantro if desired. Top with **Taste Toppers**.      *Makes 6 servings*

**Betsy Butterfly (page 157)**

What is Tex-Mex? Tex-Mex refers to food that combines the cultures of Texas and Mexico. Some common foods eaten are burritos, nachos and tacos.

# Hawaiian Chicken Sandwich

● **Prep Time:** 5 minutes   ● **Cook Time:** 10 minutes

⅓ cup *French's®* Worcestershire Sauce

⅓ cup molasses

1 pound thin sliced chicken cutlets

8 slices canned pineapple

2 slices onion, about ½-inch thick

4 hearty rolls, split in half

Lettuce leaves

### ZESTY MAYO

½ cup mayonnaise

2 tablespoons molasses

1 tablespoon *Frank's® RedHot®* Sauce or to taste

1 green onion, thinly sliced

**1.** Combine Worcestershire and molasses. Grill or broil chicken, pineapple and onion, turning once and brushing generously with molasses mixture.

**2.** Combine all ingredients for Zesty Mayo in small bowl. Spread on rolls. Arrange lettuce, chicken, pineapple and onion on top.

*Makes 4 servings*

**Tips to Stay Safe**

*Regardless of the cooking method used, always cook chicken completely. For food safety, DO NOT partially cook it and then store it to finish cooking later.*

# Corn Dogs

    **8 hot dogs**
    **8 wooden craft sticks**
    **1 package (about 16 ounces) refrigerated grand-size corn**
        **biscuits**
    **⅓ cup *French's*® *Classic Yellow*® Mustard**
    **8 slices American cheese, cut in half**

**1.** Preheat oven to 350°F. Insert 1 wooden craft stick halfway into each hot dog; set aside.

**2.** Separate biscuits. On floured board, press or roll each biscuit into a 7×4-inch oval. Spread *2 teaspoons* mustard lengthwise down center of each biscuit. Top each with 2 pieces of cheese. Place hot dog in center of biscuit. Fold top of dough over end of hot dog. Fold sides towards center enclosing hot dog. Pinch edges to seal.

**3.** Place corn dogs, seam side down, on greased baking sheet. Bake 20 to 25 minutes or until golden brown. Cool slightly before serving.                                              *Makes 4 to 8 servings*

**Tip:** Corn dogs may be made without wooden craft sticks.

Corn Dogs

# Funny Face Sandwich Melts

● **Prep Time:** 10 minutes ● **Cook Time:** 1 minute

- 2 **super-size English muffins, split and toasted**
- 8 **teaspoons** *French's*® **Honey Mustard**
- 1 **can (8 ounces) crushed pineapple, drained**
- 8 **ounces sliced smoked ham**
- 4 **slices white American or Swiss cheese**

**1.** Place English muffins, cut side up, on baking sheet. Spread each with *2 teaspoons* mustard. Arrange one-fourth of the pineapple, ham and cheese on top, dividing evenly.

**2.** Broil until cheese melts, about 1 minute. Decorate with mustard and assorted vegetables to create your own funny face.

*Makes 4 servings*

**Tyrone Turtle (page 157)**

> This sandwich is also easy to prepare in the toaster oven. Have everyone in the family do a self-portrait.

Funny Face Sandwich Melt

# Hot Dog Burritos

●Prep Time: 5 minutes  ●Cook Time: 5 minutes

　　1 can (16 ounces) pork and beans
　　8 frankfurters, sliced
　　⅓ cup ketchup
　　2 tablespoons *French's® Classic Yellow® Mustard*
　　2 tablespoons brown sugar
　　8 (8-inch) flour tortillas, heated

**1.** Combine beans, frankfurters, ketchup, mustard and brown sugar in medium saucepan. Bring to boiling over medium-high heat. Reduce heat to low and simmer 2 minutes.

**2.** Fill tortillas with bean mixture. Roll up jelly-roll style.

*Makes 8 servings*

> For extra crunch, sprinkle burritos with *French's Taste Toppers* before rolling up!

**Slinky the Snake (page 159)**

Hot Dog Burrito

# Rainbow Spirals

●●●●●●●●●●●●●●●●●●●●●●●●●●●●●●●●●●●●●●●●●●●●●●●●●●

● **Prep Time:** 10 minutes

> 4 (10-inch) flour tortillas (assorted flavors and colors)
> 4 tablespoons *French's®* Mustard (any flavor)
> ½ pound (about 8 slices) thinly sliced deli roast beef, bologna or turkey
> 8 slices American, provolone or Muenster cheese
> Fancy party toothpicks

**1.** Spread each tortilla with *1 tablespoon* mustard. Layer with meat and cheeses, dividing evenly.

**2.** Roll-up jelly-roll style; secure with toothpicks and cut into thirds. Arrange on platter.

*Makes 4 to 6 servings*

**Patrick Peacock (page 158)**

Rainbow Spirals make great party sandwiches. For added fun, put the ingredients out on the table and let everyone roll their favorite combination.

Rainbow Spirals

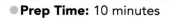

# Scrumptious Sides

## BBQ Corn Wheels

● **Prep Time:** 10 minutes    ● **Cook Time:** 10 minutes

**4 ears corn on the cob, husked and cleaned**
**3 red, green or yellow bell peppers, cut into large chunks**
**¾ cup prepared barbecue sauce**
**½ cup honey**
**¼ cup *French's®* Worcestershire Sauce**
**Vegetable cooking spray**

**1.** Cut corn into ½-inch slices. Alternately thread corn and pepper chunks onto four metal skewers. (Pierce tip of skewer through center of corn wheel to thread.) Combine barbecue sauce, honey and Worcestershire.

**2.** Coat kabobs with vegetable cooking spray. Grill kabobs on greased rack over medium heat 5 minutes. Cook 5 minutes more or until corn is tender, turning and basting with barbecue sauce mixture. Serve any extra sauce on the side with grilled hamburgers, steak or chicken.    *Makes 4 servings*

BBQ Corn Wheels

# Honey Mustard-Orange Roasted Vegetables

● **Prep Time:** 10 minutes  ● **Cook Time:** 20 minutes

  **6 cups** assorted cut-up vegetables (red or green bell
       peppers, yellow squash, red onions and carrots)
  **2 tablespoons** olive oil
  **1 teaspoon** minced garlic
  **¼ cup** *French's*® Honey Mustard
  **2 tablespoons** orange juice
  **1 teaspoon** grated orange peel

**1.** Preheat oven to 450° F. Toss vegetables with oil, garlic and
*1 teaspoon salt* in roasting pan.

**2.** Bake, uncovered, 20 minutes or until tender.

**3.** Toss vegetables with mustard, juice and orange peel just before
serving. Serve over pasta or with bread, if desired.

*Makes 6 servings*

**Penelopy Porcupine (page 160)**

> To keep little hands away from knives, buy pre-cut vegetables at your local grocery store salad bar. It also saves time for an even quicker dish.

Honey Mustard-Orange Roasted Vegetables

# Quick 'N' Easy Home-Style Beans

●**Prep Time:** 5 minutes　　●**Cook Time:** 5 minutes

　　**2 cans (16 ounces each) pork and beans**
　**¼ cup *French's® Classic Yellow®* Mustard**
　**¼ cup packed light brown sugar**
　　**2 tablespoons *French's®* Worcestershire Sauce**
　**1½ cups shredded Cheddar cheese**
　**1½ cups *French's® Taste Toppers*™ French Fried Onions**

**1.** Combine beans, mustard, sugar and Worcestershire in medium skillet. Cook over medium heat until hot and bubbly.

**2.** Top with cheese and **Taste Toppers**. Cover and cook until cheese melts.

**3.** Serve with grilled or broiled hot dogs.　　　*Makes 6 servings*

**Tip:** For more fun, create one of the following funny shape hot dogs:

● Cut diagonal slits ½-inch apart down length of each hot dog, cutting almost all the way through. Grill or boil; hot dog will fan open when cooking.

● Make about 6 criss-cross slits, ½-inch in from ends of each hot dog. Grill.

● Cut four slits ¼-inch apart into the side of each hot dog. Turn hot dog so that the cuts are on the opposite side. Make four more cuts. Repeat turning and cutting down length of hot dog. Hot dogs will open up when broiled.

# Cheddary Garlic Mashed Potatoes

● **Prep Time:** 5 minutes    ● **Cook Time:** 10 minutes

  4 **cups hot mashed potatoes**

  1 **can (10¾ ounces) condensed cream of chicken soup**

1½ **cups shredded Cheddar cheese**

  ⅛ **teaspoon garlic powder**

1½ **cups** *French's® Taste Toppers™* **French Fried Onions**

**1.** Preheat oven to 375°F. Heat mashed potatoes, soup, *1 cup* cheese and garlic powder in saucepan over medium heat. Stir until cheese melts.

**2.** Spoon potato mixture into 2-quart baking dish. Top with *½ cup* cheese and **Taste Toppers**.

**3.** Bake 5 to 10 minutes or until hot and until onions are golden.

*Makes 6 to 8 servings*

No time to make mashed potatoes? Prepare instant mashed potatoes for 8 servings using 2⅔ cups instant potatoes.

**Happy Hot Dog (page 160)**

# Macaroni & Cheese Boats

**Prep Time:** 10 minutes     **Cook Time:** 7 minutes

  1 box (7.25 ounces) macaroni & cheese mix
  ¼ cup milk
  ¼ cup butter
1½ cups shredded Cheddar cheese, divided
  1 tablespoon *French's®* Worcestershire Sauce
  4 red, green or yellow bell peppers, halved lengthwise
1⅓ cups *French's®* Taste Toppers™ French Fried Onions

**1.** Prepare macaroni & cheese in medium saucepan as directed on package using ¼ cup milk and ¼ cup butter. Stir in *1 cup* cheese and Worcestershire; set aside.

**2.** Arrange peppers cut side up in glass baking dish. Add *¼ cup water* to baking dish and cover. Microwave on HIGH 5 minutes or until crisp-tender; drain.

**3.** Spoon macaroni & cheese into peppers and sprinkle with remaining cheese. Sprinkle with **Taste Toppers** and microwave 2 minutes.

*Makes 4 servings*

### Tips to Stay Safe

Remember, adults should always help kids use the oven, stove top, microwave, electric blender and sharp knives to avoid any injuries.

Macaroni & Cheese Boats

# Zippy Oven Fries

● **Prep Time:** 10 minutes ● **Cook Time:** 25 minutes

  1 **pound russet potatoes, sliced into ¼-inch wedges**
  3 **tablespoons hot melted butter or vegetable oil**
  2 **tablespoons _Frank's® RedHot®_ Sauce, at room temperature**
  2 **cups _French's® Taste Toppers™_ French Fried Onions, finely crushed**
  ½ **cup grated Parmesan cheese**
    **Zesty Ketchup (recipe follows)**

**1.** Preheat oven to 400°F. Place potatoes, butter and **RedHot** Sauce in large resealable plastic bag. Seal bag and toss potatoes to coat.

**2.** Combine **Taste Toppers** and cheese on sheet of waxed paper. Coat potatoes in crumb mixture, pressing firmly.

**3.** Arrange potatoes in single layer in shallow baking pan coated with nonstick cooking spray. Bake, uncovered, 25 minutes or until potatoes are tender and golden brown. Splash on more **RedHot** Sauce or serve with Zesty Ketchup. _Makes 4 servings_

**Zesty Ketchup:** Combine 1 cup ketchup with 1 to 2 tablespoons **RedHot** Sauce.

Zippy Oven Fries

# Zesty Corn Sauté

● **Prep Time:** 5 minutes   ● **Cook Time:** 7 minutes

- ½ cup finely chopped onion
- ½ cup finely chopped red or green bell pepper
- 1 bag (16 ounces) frozen sweet corn
- 1 tablespoon *Frank's® RedHot®* Sauce
- 1 teaspoon chili powder

**1.** Heat *2 tablespoons oil* in 12-inch nonstick skillet over medium-high heat. Cook onion and pepper 4 minutes or until tender, stirring occasionally.

**2.** Stir in corn, **RedHot** Sauce and chili powder. Simmer over medium heat 3 minutes or until corn is heated through. Garnish, if desired, with chopped green onion. Splash on more **RedHot** Sauce to taste.

*Makes 4 to 6 servings*

# Sweet & Tangy Coleslaw

● **Prep Time:** 5 minutes

- 1 small bag (16 ounces) shredded cabbage
- ½ cup mayonnaise
- ½ cup *French's®* Honey Mustard

**1.** Combine ingredients in medium bowl. Chill until ready to serve.

*Makes 6 to 8 servings*

# Cheesy Vegetable Casserole

● **Prep Time:** 5 minutes    ● **Cook Time:** 35 minutes

> 1 can (10¾ ounces) condensed Cheddar cheese soup
> 2 cups shredded Cheddar cheese
> ½ cup sour cream
> ¼ cup milk
> 1 bag (16 ounces) frozen vegetable combination, thawed and drained
> 1½ cups *French's® Taste Toppers™* French Fried Onions

**1.** Preheat oven to 350°F. Combine soup, *1 cup* cheese, sour cream and milk in 2-quart baking dish. Stir in vegetables.

**2.** Bake, uncovered, 30 minutes or until hot; stir.

**3.** Top with remaining *1 cup* cheese and **Taste Toppers**. Bake 5 minutes or until golden.                    *Makes 6 servings*

**Microwave Directions:** Prepare vegetable mixture as above. Cover with vented plastic wrap. Microwave on HIGH 10 minutes or until hot, stirring halfway. Top with cheese and **Taste Toppers**. Microwave 2 minutes or until golden.

**Rodney Rooster (page 159)**

Vegetables have never tasted so good! Let your kids pick their favorite vegetables for this lip-smacking dish.

**Scrumptious Sides** **133**

# Sunshine Citrus Salad

●**Prep Time:** 5 minutes

8 cups washed and torn mixed salad greens
2 oranges, peeled and cut into sections
1 cup sliced strawberries or grapes
¼ cup coconut
¼ cup toasted almonds
Sunshine Citrus Dressing (recipe follows)

**1.** Arrange all ingredients on serving plates, dividing evenly. Serve with Sunshine Citrus Dressing.                    *Makes 4 servings*

# Sunshine Citrus Dressing

●**Prep Time:** 5 minutes

½ cup orange juice
2 tablespoons *French's*® Honey Mustard
2 tablespoons oil
2 tablespoons red wine vinegar
2 to 3 teaspoons *Frank's*® *RedHot*® Sauce

**1.** Combine all ingredients in small bowl.

*Makes about 1 cup dressing*

**Tip:** To turn this side dish into a main dish, simply add leftover cooked chicken.

Sunshine Citrus Salad

# Mediterranean Strata

● **Prep Time:** 15 minutes    ● **Cook Time:** about 1 hour

2 pounds green zucchini or yellow squash, cut into ¼-inch slices

1 cup ricotta cheese

3 eggs

1½ cups milk, heavy cream or half and half

1 cup minced fresh basil (2 bunches)

2 tablespoons all-purpose flour

1 tablespoon minced garlic

1 cup shredded mozzarella cheese

1⅓ cups *French's® Taste Toppers™ French Fried Onions*

**1.** Preheat oven to 350°F. Place zucchini and *2 tablespoons water* into 2-quart microwave-safe baking dish. Cover with vented plastic wrap. Microwave on HIGH 3 minutes or until just tender; drain well.

**2.** Whisk together ricotta cheese, eggs, milk, basil, flour, garlic and *½ teaspoon* salt in large bowl. Pour over zucchini in baking dish. Sprinkle with cheese. Bake, uncovered, 45 minutes or until custard is just set.

**3.** Sprinkle with mozzarella cheese and **Taste Toppers**. Bake 5 minutes or until onions are golden. Garnish with diced red bell pepper, if desired.                    *Makes 6 servings*

**Note:** A strata is a dish that is typically made by layering ingredients and then baking. It is often made of eggs, bread, cheese and combinations of other ingredients. Stratas can be a breakfast dish, a main dish or even a side dish.

Mediterranean Strata

# Asian Chicken Salad

● **Prep Time:** 10 minutes  ● **Cook Time:** 15 minutes

   4 **boneless skinless chicken breast halves**
       **Asian Dressing & Marinade (recipe follows)**
   8 **cups torn iceberg or Romaine lettuce**
   1 **large carrot, shredded**
1⅓ **cups** *French's® Taste Toppers™* **French Fried Onions**

**1.** Place chicken in resealable plastic food storage bag. Pour half the Asian Dressing & Marinade over chicken. Seal bag; refrigerate 30 minutes. Reserve remaining Asian Dressing & Marinade.

**2.** Grill or broil chicken 15 minutes or until no longer pink in center. Cut chicken into diagonal slices.

**3.** Arrange lettuce on serving platter and top with carrot. Arrange sliced chicken breast on top and drizzle with reserved Asian Dressing & Marinade. Sprinkle with **Taste Toppers**.

*Makes 4 servings*

# Asian Dressing & Marinade

● **Prep Time:** 5 minutes

   ⅓ **cup** *French's®* **Worcestershire Sauce**
   ⅓ **cup red wine vinegar**
   ⅓ **cup honey**
   ¼ **cup vegetable oil**
   1 **tablespoon** *French's®* **Dijon Mustard**
   ¼ **teaspoon ground ginger**

**1.** Combine all ingredients in medium bowl.

*Makes about 1¼ cups*

**138** *Scrumptious Sides*

# Cheddar Broccoli Potatoes

●**Prep Time:** 20 minutes  ●**Cook Time:** 2 minutes

    6 hot baked potatoes, split open lengthwise
 1½ cups chopped, cooked broccoli
 1⅓ cups *French's® Taste Toppers™* French Fried Onions
  ¾ cup pasteurized processed American cheese sauce, melted

**1.** Place potatoes on microwave-safe dish. Scrape cooked potato with fork to fluff up. Top with broccoli and **Taste Toppers**, dividing evenly.

**2.** Microwave on HIGH 2 minutes or until onions are golden.

**3.** Drizzle melted cheese sauce on top.        *Makes 6 servings*

# Honey Mustard Glazed Vegetables

●**Prep Time:** 5 minutes   ●**Cook Time:** 7 minutes

    2 tablespoons butter
    1 package (10 ounces) frozen baby carrots, thawed
 1½ cups frozen pearl onions
  ¼ cup *French's®* Honey Mustard
    2 tablespoons sugar
    1 tablespoon finely chopped parsley (optional)

**1.** Melt butter in 12-inch nonstick skillet over medium-high heat. Sauté carrots and onions 5 minutes or until crisp-tender.

**2.** Stir in mustard and sugar. Cook, stirring occationally, about 2 minutes or until vegetables are glazed. Sprinkle with parsley, if desired.        *Makes 4 servings*

# Dynamite Dinners

## Orange Chicken Piccata

● **Prep time:** 5 minutes  ● **Cook Time:** 10 minutes

**1 pound boneless skinless chicken
  breasts, pounded thin**
**2 tablespoons all-purpose flour**
**½ cup orange juice**
**¼ cup *French's*® Honey Mustard**
**¼ cup orange marmalade**
**¼ teaspoon dried rosemary leaves,
  crushed**
**1 orange, thinly sliced and quartered**

**1.** Coat chicken with flour; shake off excess. Heat *1 tablespoon oil* in nonstick skillet over medium-high heat. Cook chicken 5 minutes or until browned.

**2.** Mix orange juice, mustard, marmalade and rosemary. Add to skillet. Bring to boiling. Simmer, uncovered, over medium-low heat 5 minutes or until chicken is no longer pink in center and sauce thickens slightly. Stir in orange pieces; heat through. Serve with rice, if desired. *Makes 4 servings*

Orange Chicken Piccata

# Zesty Mexican Stir-Fry Fajitas

- 1 **pound beef sirloin, flank or round steak, thinly sliced**
- 1 **large red bell pepper, thinly sliced**
- 1 **medium onion, sliced**
- 1 **jar (12 ounces) prepared beef gravy**
- 2 **tablespoons *Frank's® RedHot®* Sauce or to taste**
- 1 **teaspoon garlic powder**
- 1 **teaspoon dried oregano leaves**
- 1 **teaspoon ground cumin**
- 8 **flour tortillas, heated**

**1.** Heat *2 tablespoons oil* in large skillet over high heat until hot. Stir-fry beef in batches 5 minutes or until browned.

**2.** Add pepper and onion; cook 2 minutes. Add remaining ingredients except tortillas. Stir-fry an additional 2 minutes. Spoon mixture into tortillas; roll up. Splash on more **RedHot** Sauce to taste.

*Makes 4 servings*

**Harriet Ham Sandwich**
**(page 160)**

Mix it up! If you serve this zesty recipe with tortillas, serve any leftovers over rice.

Zesty Mexican Stir-Fry Fajitas

# Pizza Pie Meatloaf

●**Prep Time:** 10 minutes     ●**Cook Time:** 40 minutes

        2 **pounds ground beef**
    1½ **cups shredded mozzarella cheese**
     ½ **cup unseasoned dry bread crumbs**
      1 **cup tomato sauce**
     ¼ **cup grated Parmesan cheese**
     ¼ **cup *French's*® Worcestershire Sauce**
      1 **tablespoon dried oregano leaves**
    1⅓ **cups *French's*® *Taste Toppers*™ French Fried Onions**

**1.** Preheat oven to 350°F. Combine beef, ½ *cup* mozzarella, bread crumbs, ½ *cup* tomato sauce, Parmesan cheese, Worcestershire and oregano in large bowl; stir with fork until well blended.

**2.** Place meat mixture into round pizza pan with edge or pie plate and shape into 9×1-inch round. Bake 35 minutes or until no longer pink in center and internal temperature reads 160°F. Drain fat.

**3.** Top with remaining tomato sauce, sliced tomato and green bell pepper strips, remaining mozzarella cheese and ***Taste Toppers***. Bake 5 minutes or until cheese is melted and ***Taste Toppers*** are golden. Cut into wedges to serve.     *Makes 6 to 8 servings*

Pizza Pie Meatloaf

# Glazed Pork Chops & Apples

● **Prep Time:** 5 minutes    ● **Cook Time:** 13 minutes

    4 boneless pork chops, ½ inch thick
    ½ cup apple juice
    ¼ cup *French's*® Hearty Deli Mustard
    ¼ cup packed brown sugar
    1 red or green apple, cut into small chunks

**1.** Heat *1 tablespoon oil* in large nonstick skillet over medium-high heat. Cook pork chops 5 minutes or until browned on both sides.

**2.** Add remaining ingredients. Bring to boiling. Reduce heat to medium. Simmer, uncovered, 8 to 10 minutes or until pork is no longer pink in center and sauce thickens slightly, stirring occasionally.

**3.** Serve with noodles, if desired.              *Makes 4 servings*


# Honey-Lime Chicken

● **Prep Time:** 10 minutes    ● **Cook Time:** 12 minutes

    1 pound boneless skinless chicken breast halves, cut into
        1-inch cubes
    1 cup chopped red bell pepper
    1 cup thinly sliced carrots
    ¼ cup *French's*® Dijon Mustard
    ¼ cup honey
    ¼ cup lime juice
    ¼ cup orange juice

**1.** Heat *1 tablespoon oil* in nonstick skillet over medium-high heat. Cook chicken and vegetables 10 minutes or until chicken is no longer pink in center and vegetables are crisp-tender.

**2.** Add remaining ingredients; bring to boiling. Cook until sauce thickens slightly, stirring occasionally. Serve over rice, if desired.

*Makes 4 servings*

Glazed Pork Chop & Apples

# Mini Chicken Pot Pies

● **Prep Time:** 15 minutes  ● **Cook Time:** about 20 minutes

1 container (about 16 ounces) refrigerated reduced-fat
    buttermilk biscuits

1½ cups milk

1 package (1.8 ounces) white sauce mix

2 cups cut-up cooked chicken

1 cup frozen assorted vegetables, partially thawed

2 cups shredded Cheddar cheese

2 cups *French's® Taste Toppers™* French Fried Onions

**1.** Preheat oven to 400°F. Separate biscuits; press into 8 (8-ounce) custard cups, pressing up sides to form crust.

**2.** Whisk milk and sauce mix in medium saucepan. Bring to boiling over medium-high heat. Reduce heat to medium-low; simmer 1 minute, whisking constantly, until thickened. Stir in chicken and vegetables.

**3.** Spoon about ⅓ cup chicken mixture into each crust. Place cups on baking sheet. Bake 15 minutes or until golden brown. Top each with cheese and **Taste Toppers**. Bake 3 minutes or until golden.

*Makes 8 servings*

Mini Chicken Pot Pies

# Zippy Hot Doggity Tacos

● **Prep Time:** 5 minutes    ● **Cook Time:** 8 minutes

1 small onion, finely chopped

1 tablespoon *Frank's® RedHot®* Sauce or *French's®*
    Worcestershire Sauce

4 frankfurters, chopped

1 can (10½ ounces) black beans or red kidney beans, drained

1 can (8 ounces) tomato sauce

1 teaspoon chili powder

8 taco shells, heated

Toppings: chopped tomatoes, shredded lettuce, sliced
    olives, sour cream, shredded cheese

1 cup *French's® Taste Toppers™* French Fried Onions

**1.** Heat *1 tablespoon oil* in 12-inch nonstick skillet over medium-high heat. Cook onion, 3 minutes or until crisp-tender. Stir in remaining ingredients. Bring to boiling. Reduce heat to medium-low and cook 5 minutes, stirring occasionally.

**2.** To serve, spoon chili into taco shells. Garnish as desired and sprinkle with **Taste Toppers**. Splash on **RedHot** Sauce for extra zip!

*Makes 4 servings*

Zippy Hot Doggity Tacos

# Grilled Chicken Stix

● **Prep Time:** 10 minutes  ● **Cook Time:** 5 minutes

> 1 **pound thin sliced chicken breast cutlets**
> 12 **to 14 wooden skewers, soaked in water**
> 2 **oranges, cut into eighths**
> ½ **cup prepared barbecue sauce**
> ½ **cup honey**
> 3 **tablespoons *Frank's® RedHot®* Sauce**
> **Spicy Cucumber Salsa (recipe follows)**

**1.** Slice cutlets into ½-inch wide long strips. Weave strips onto upper half of 8 to 10 skewers. Place skewers into large baking dish. Thread 4 orange pieces each onto remaining 4 skewers. Set aside.

**2.** Combine barbecue sauce, honey and **RedHot** sauce in measuring cup. Reserve ¼ *cup* mixture for Spicy Cucumber Salsa. Pour ½ *cup* of remaining mixture over chicken, turning skewers to coat.

**3.** Grill or broil chicken and oranges 5 minutes or until chicken is no longer pink in center and oranges are heated through. Turn and baste chicken often with remaining ½ *cup* barbecue sauce mixture. Serve with Spicy Cucumber Salsa.  *Makes 4 servings*

# Spicy Cucumber Salsa

● **Prep Time:** 10 minutes

> 1 **large cucumber, peeled, seeded and chopped**
> 1 **small red bell pepper, finely chopped**
> ¼ **cup finely chopped red onion**
> 2 **tablespoons finely chopped fresh cilantro or parsley**
> **Reserved ¼ cup barbecue sauce mixture**

**1.** Combine all ingredients in large bowl; chill. Serve with Grilled Chicken Stix or your favorite grilled chicken or steak recipe.
*Makes 4 to 6 servings (about 2 cups)*

Grilled Chicken Stix and Spicy Cucumber Salsa

# Sweet & Zesty Fish with Fruit Salsa

● **Prep Time:** 10 minutes　　● **Cook Time:** 8 minutes

- ¼ cup *French's*® Hearty Deli Brown Mustard
- ¼ cup **honey**
- 2 cups **chopped assorted fresh fruit (pineapple, kiwi, strawberries and mango)**
- 1 pound **sea bass or cod fillets or other firm-fleshed white fish**

**1.** Preheat broiler or grill. Combine mustard and honey. Stir *2 tablespoons* mustard mixture into fruit; set aside.

**2.** Brush remaining mustard mixture on both sides of fillets. Place in foil-lined broiler pan. Broil or grill fish 6 inches from heat 8 minutes or until fish is opaque.

**3.** Serve fruit salsa with fish.　　　　*Makes 4 servings*

**Tip:** To prepare this meal even faster, purchase cut-up fresh fruit from the salad bar.

Tips to Stay Safe

**Hand check! Don't forget to use hot pads when handling anything that is warm or hot.**

Sweet & Zesty Fish with Fruit Salsa

# Yummy Weeknight Chicken

●**Prep Time:** 10 minutes ●**Cook Time:** 12 minutes

- **1 pound boneless skinless chicken breasts, pounded thin**
- **1 small onion, sliced**
- **1 package (10 ounces) mushrooms, sliced**
- **⅓ cup barbecue sauce**
- **¼ cup honey**
- **2 tablespoons *French's*® Worcestershire Sauce**

**1.** Heat *1 tablespoon oil* in large nonstick skillet over medium-high heat. Cook chicken 5 minutes or until chicken is no longer pink in center. Remove chicken to serving platter; keep warm.

**2.** In same skillet, cook onion and mushrooms, stirring occasionally, 5 minutes or until mushrooms are golden brown and no liquid remains. Return chicken to skillet.

**3.** Combine remaining ingredients. Pour into skillet. Bring to boiling. Reduce heat and cook 2 to 3 minutes until sauce thickens slightly, stirring occasionally. Serve with hot cooked rice, if desired.

*Makes 4 servings*

**Tips to Stay Safe**

**Wash up! Be sure to always thoroughly wash cutting surfaces, utensils and your hands with hot soapy water after handling uncooked chicken.**

# Funny Face Factory

## Betsy Butterfly

Trim crust of bread slice to resemble curves of butterfly wings. Arrange slices of salami and pepperoni on top of bread to form wings. Use slender carrot stick or red bell pepper slice for body. Cut green portion of green onion for antennae; insert under salami. Cut slices of jalapeño peppers or green olives for spots on wings. Decorate with ketchup and French's mustard as desired.

## Tish the Fish

Squeeze French's mustard in curls on cooked breaded chicken drumstick to resemble scales. Arrange green onion slice and black olive piece for eye. Place a small red bell pepper slice on drumstick for mouth. Arrange red or orange bell pepper slices for tail and fins.

## Tyrone Turtle

Shape ground beef into an oval patty; cook until well done. Spread ketchup on bottom of toasted English muffin; top with cooked hamburger patty. Squeeze French's mustard on top of patty to resemble markings of a turtle shell. Cut small dill pickles in half lengthwise for head and legs. Cut red bell pepper pieces for tail and eyes.

## Pierre Pretzel

Thaw frozen soft pretzels according to package directions. Place slices of radishes and black olives for eyes. Cut baby eggplant in half lengthwise for hat. Cut remaining eggplant in half into bow-tie. Place a piece of radish for detail on bow-tie. Cut small slits into flattened black olive halves for the mustache. Squeeze French's mustard to make mouth and eyebrow.

## Nosey Nick

Cook hamburger patty until well done. Place on bottom of hamburger bun. Cut American cheese into a triangle to form hat. Add red bell pepper slice for band on hat. Place slices of radish and black olives on hamburger patty for eyes. Break crisp breadstick into 3-inch long piece; insert into hamburger for nose. Squeeze French's mustard for smile. Use a piece of green leaf lettuce for hair and a piece of red cabbage for the feather in his hat.

## Patrick Peacock

Roll assorted deli meats and cheeses to form feathers of peacock as shown in photo. Place red and green bell pepper strips between slices of meat and cheese. Decorate with French's mustard and olive slices. Cut a slice of apple into head and body of peacock as shown in photo. Squeeze French's mustard to form legs and feet.

## Davey Dinosaur

Press an unbaked breadstick into a lightly greased round baking dish to form a slight curve. Bake according to package directions. Cut out 4 triangular pieces from one side of frankfurter or knockwurst. Cook in boiling water about 2 minutes until curved. Place breadstick on plate. Lay cooked frankfurter, cut-out side up, beside breadstick. Cut a crisp breadstick for legs. Cut a triangle of Cheddar cheese for horn, slice of green olive for eye and slice of red bell pepper for mouth. Cut a cucumber to create the tail. Squeeze French's mustard to decorate.

## Slinky the Snake

Cook a regular and jumbo-size frankfurter as desired. Cut each frankfurter into ½-inch slices. Cut cucumber and carrot into ⅛-inch slices. Alternate frankfurter slices, carrot slices and cucumber slices on plate as shown in photo. Cut cucumber wedge for tail. Squeeze 2 dots of French's Mustard on first frankfurter slice for eyes. Place a caper or dill pickle pieces in center of eyes. Cut red bell pepper to form forked tongue. Squeeze French's mustard onto snake for spots.

## School Bus

Cut 2 slices of white bread into bus shape; fill as desired. Spread top of sandwich with French's mustard. Squeeze French's mustard around bus shape as shown in photo. Use black olive halves for windows and cucumber pieces for front and back bumper. Place green grape half for headlight and cherry tomato half for taillight. Cut slices of cherry pepper and pepperoni for wheels.

## Rodney Rooster

Fill ramekin with French's mustard and place in center of serving plate. Bake 4 chicken nuggets according to package directions. Place 1 nugget on top of ramekin for feather and 1 nugget for head. Cut 2 chicken nuggets in half. Arrange on serving plate alternating red bell pepper strips for feathers and tail as shown in photo. Cut small red and green bell pepper pieces for crown. Cut small black olive piece for eye and Cheddar cheese for beak. Squeeze French's mustard for legs and feather lines on nuggets.

Smile! You've got
**French's**
since 1904

### Harry Hound

Place cooked breaded chicken drumstick on plate for head. Arrange curled potato chips next to head to form ears. Place a red maraschino cherry half on drumstick for nose. Cut diagonal slices from white portion of green onion to form eyes. Place black olive pieces in center of green onion for pupils. Squeeze French's mustard for mouth.

### Penelopy Porcupine

Combine 1 package (8 ounces) cream cheese, 1 tablespoon French's® Hearty Deli Brown Mustard and 1 teaspoon French's® Worcestershire Sauce in medium bowl until well blended. Shape mixture into an oval with one end smaller for head of porcupine. Snip end of celery stick with kitchen scissors and place in ice water. Once curled, insert into cheese ball for tail. Insert French's® Potato Sticks into cheese mixture, with ends pointing slightly back, to cover everything but the head. Cut a small red bell pepper piece for nose and insert whole cloves for claws and eyes.

### Happy Hot Dog

Place grilled hot dog in hot dog bun. Squeeze French's mustard on hot dog for smile. Place two zucchini slices and black olive halves on bun for eyes. Cut small black olive slices for eye lashes.

### Harriet Ham Sandwich

Place slices of deli ham on a slice of white bread. Arrange green onion curls at top for hair. Squeeze French's mustard on ham for nose and eyes. Cut a small piece of zucchini into two triangles. Place under mustard for pupil. Cut a red bell pepper piece into a bow and place in her hair and cut a red bell pepper slice for her lips.

Cupcakes!

Over 20 Party Ideas

# Cupcakes!

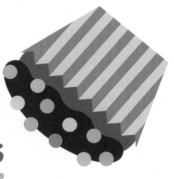
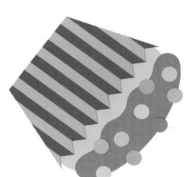

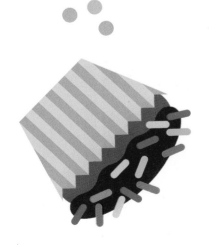

## Angel Almond Cupcakes

· · · · · · · · · · · · · · · · · · · · · · · · · · · · · · · · · · · · · · · · · · ·

    **1  package DUNCAN HINES® Angel Food Cake Mix**
**1¼  cups water**
    **2  teaspoons almond extract**
    **1  container DUNCAN HINES® Wild Cherry Vanilla Frosting**

Preheat oven to 350°F.

Combine cake mix, water and almond extract in large mixing bowl. Beat at low speed with electric mixer until moistened. Beat at medium speed for 1 minute. Line medium muffin pans with paper baking cups. Fill muffin cups two-thirds full. Bake 20 to 25 minutes or until golden brown, cracked and dry. Remove from muffin pans. Cool completely. Frost with frosting.       *Makes 30 to 32 cupcakes*

Angel Almond Cupcakes

# Peanut Butter Mini Muffins

. . . . . . . . . . . . . . . . . . . .

- ⅓ cup creamy peanut butter
- ¼ cup (½ stick) butter, softened
- ¼ cup granulated sugar
- ¼ cup firmly packed light brown sugar
- 1 large egg
- ¾ cup buttermilk
- 3 tablespoons vegetable oil
- ¾ teaspoon vanilla extract
- 1½ cups all-purpose flour
- ¾ teaspoon baking powder
- ½ teaspoon baking soda
- ½ teaspoon salt
- 1¼ cups "M&M's"® Milk Chocolate Mini Baking Bits, divided

  Chocolate Glaze (recipe follows)

Preheat oven to 350°F. Lightly grease 36 (1¾-inch) mini muffin cups or line with paper or foil liners; set aside. In large bowl cream peanut butter, butter and sugars until light and fluffy; beat in egg. Beat in buttermilk, oil and vanilla. In medium bowl combine flour, baking powder, baking soda and salt; gradually blend into creamed mixture. Divide batter evenly among prepared muffin cups. Sprinkle batter evenly with ¾ cup "M&M's"® Milk Chocolate Mini Baking Bits. Bake 15 to 17 minutes or until toothpick inserted in centers comes out clean. Cool completely on wire racks. Prepare Chocolate Glaze. Place glaze in resealable plastic sandwich bag; seal bag. Cut tiny piece off one corner of bag (not more than ⅛ inch). Drizzle glaze over muffins. Decorate with remaining ½ cup "M&M's"® Milk Chocolate Mini Baking Bits. Store in tightly covered container.

*Makes 3 dozen mini muffins*

**Chocolate Glaze:** In top of double boiler over hot water melt 2 (1-ounce) squares semi-sweet chocolate and 1 tablespoon butter. Stir until smooth; let cool slightly.

**Peanut Butter Mini Muffins**

# Blueberry Crisp Cupcakes

## Cupcakes
- 2 cups all-purpose flour
- 2 teaspoons baking powder
- ¼ teaspoon salt
- 1¾ cups granulated sugar
- ½ cup (1 stick) butter, softened
- ¾ cup milk
- 1½ teaspoons vanilla
- 3 large egg whites
- 3 cups fresh or frozen (unthawed) blueberries

## Streusel
- ⅓ cup all-purpose flour
- ¼ cup quick or old-fashioned oats, uncooked
- ¼ cup packed light brown sugar
- ½ teaspoon ground cinnamon
- ¼ cup butter, softened
- ½ cup chopped walnuts or pecans

**1.** Preheat oven to 350°F. Line 30 regular-size (2½-inch) muffin cups with paper muffin cup liners.

**2.** For cupcakes, combine 2 cups flour, baking powder and salt in medium bowl; mix well and set aside. Beat granulated sugar and ½ cup butter with electric mixer at medium speed 1 minute. Add milk and vanilla. Beat at low speed 30 seconds. Gradually beat in flour mixture; beat at medium speed 2 minutes.

Add egg whites; beat 1 minute. Spoon batter into prepared muffin cups filling ½ full. Spoon blueberries over batter. Bake 10 minutes.

**3.** Meanwhile for streusel, combine ⅓ cup flour, oats, brown sugar and cinnamon in small bowl; mix well. Cut in butter with pastry blender or two knives until mixture is well combined. Stir in chopped nuts.

**4.** Sprinkle streusel over partially baked cupcakes. Return to oven; bake 18 to 20 minutes or until golden brown and toothpick inserted into centers comes out clean. Cool in pans on wire racks 10 minutes. Remove cupcakes to racks; cool completely. (Cupcakes may be frozen up to 3 months.)

*Makes 30 cupcakes*

# Coconut Cupcakes

1 package DUNCAN HINES® Moist Deluxe Butter Recipe Golden Cake Mix
3 eggs
1 cup (8 ounces) dairy sour cream
⅔ cup cream of coconut
¼ cup butter or margarine, softened
2 containers (16 ounces each) DUNCAN HINES® Cream Cheese Frosting
2½ cups toasted coconut (see Tip)

1. Preheat oven to 375°F. Place 36 (2½-inch) paper liners in muffin cups.

2. Combine cake mix, eggs, sour cream, cream of coconut and butter in large bowl. Beat at low speed until blended. Beat at medium speed 4 minutes. Fill paper liners half full. Bake 17 to 19 minutes or until toothpick inserted in center comes out clean. Cool in pans 5 minutes. Remove to cooling racks. Cool completely.

3. Frost cupcakes; sprinkle with toasted coconut.

*Makes 36 cupcakes*

**Tip:** To toast coconut, spread evenly on baking sheet. Toast in 350°F oven for 3 minutes. Stir and toast 1 to 2 minutes longer or until light golden brown.

# Cookies & Cream Cupcakes

2¼ cups all-purpose flour
1 tablespoon baking powder
½ teaspoon salt
1⅔ cups sugar
½ cup (1 stick) butter, softened
1 cup milk
2 teaspoons vanilla
3 egg whites
1 cup crushed chocolate sandwich cookies (about 10 cookies) plus additional for garnish
1 container (16 ounces) vanilla frosting

1. Preheat oven to 350°F. Line 24 (2½-inch) muffin cups with paper muffin cup liners.

2. Sift flour, baking powder and salt together in large bowl. Stir in sugar. Add butter, milk and vanilla; beat with electric mixer at low speed 30 seconds. Beat at medium speed 2 minutes. Add egg whites; beat 2 minutes. Stir in 1 cup crushed cookies.

3. Spoon batter into prepared pans. Bake 20 to 25 minutes or until toothpick inserted into centers comes out clean. Cool in pans on wire racks 10 minutes. Remove to racks; cool.

4. Frost cupcakes; garnish with additional crushed cookies.

*Makes 24 cupcakes*

# Glazed Cranberry Mini-Cakes

- ⅓ cup butter or margarine, softened
- ⅓ cup granulated sugar
- ⅓ cup packed light brown sugar
- 1 egg
- 1¼ teaspoons vanilla extract
- 1⅓ cups all-purpose flour
- ¾ teaspoon baking powder
- ¼ teaspoon baking soda
- ¼ teaspoon salt
- 2 tablespoons milk
- 1¼ cups coarsely chopped fresh cranberries
- ½ cup coarsely chopped walnuts
- 1⅔ cups HERSHEY'S Premier White Chips, divided
- White Glaze (recipe follows)

**1.** Heat oven to 350°F. Lightly grease or paper-line small muffin cups (1¾ inches in diameter).

**2.** Beat butter, granulated sugar, brown sugar, egg and vanilla in large bowl until fluffy. Stir together flour, baking powder, baking soda and salt; gradually blend into butter mixture. Add milk; stir until blended. Stir in cranberries, walnuts and ⅔ cup white chips (reserve remaining chips for glaze). Fill muffin cups ⅞ full with batter.

**3.** Bake 18 to 20 minutes or until wooden pick inserted in center comes out clean. Cool 5 minutes; remove from pans to wire rack. Cool completely. Prepare White Glaze; drizzle over top of mini-cakes. Refrigerate 10 minutes to set glaze. *Makes about 3 dozen mini-cakes*

**White Glaze:** Place remaining 1 cup HERSHEY'S Premier White Chips in small microwave-safe bowl; sprinkle 2 tablespoons vegetable oil over chips. Microwave at HIGH (100% power) 30 seconds; stir. If necessary, microwave at HIGH additional 30 seconds or just until chips are melted when stirred.

# Double Malted Cupcakes

**Cupcakes**
- 2 cups all-purpose flour
- ¼ cup malted milk powder
- 2 teaspoons baking powder
- ¼ teaspoon salt
- 1¾ cups granulated sugar
- ½ cup (1 stick) butter, softened
- 1 cup 2% or whole milk
- 1½ teaspoons vanilla
- 3 large egg whites

**Frosting**
- 4 ounces milk chocolate candy bar, broken into chunks
- ¼ cup (½ stick) butter
- ¼ cup whipping cream
- 1 tablespoon malted milk powder
- 1 teaspoon vanilla
- 1¾ cups powdered sugar
- 30 chocolate-covered malt ball candies

**1.** Preheat oven to 350°F. Line 30 regular-size (2½-inch) muffin cups with paper muffin cup liners.

**2.** For cupcakes, combine flour, ¼ cup malted milk powder, baking powder and salt; mix well and set aside. Beat sugar and ½ cup butter with electric mixer at medium speed 1 minute. Add milk and 1½ teaspoons vanilla. Beat at low speed 30 seconds. Gradually beat in flour mixture; beat at medium speed 2 minutes. Add egg whites; beat 1 minute.

**3.** Spoon batter into prepared muffin cups filling ⅔ full. Bake 20 minutes or until golden brown and toothpick inserted into center comes out clean. Cool in pans on wire racks 10 minutes. (Center of cupcakes will sink slightly upon cooling.) Remove cupcakes to racks; cool completely. (At this point, cupcakes may be frozen up to 3 months.)

**4.** For frosting, melt chocolate and ¼ cup butter in heavy medium saucepan over low heat, stirring frequently. Stir in cream, 1 tablespoon malted milk powder and 1 teaspoon vanilla; mix well. Gradually stir in powdered sugar. Cook 4 to 5 minutes, stirring constantly, until small lumps disappear. Remove from heat. Chill 20 minutes, beating every 5 minutes until frosting is spreadable.

**5.** Spread cooled cupcakes with frosting; decorate with chocolate covered malt ball candies. Store at room temperature up to 24 hours or cover and refrigerate for up to 3 days before serving.

*Makes 30 cupcakes*

# Lemon Poppy Seed Cupcakes

**CUPCAKES**
- 1 package DUNCAN HINES® Moist Deluxe Lemon Supreme Cake Mix
- 3 eggs
- 1⅓ cups water
- ⅓ cup vegetable oil
- 3 tablespoons poppy seed

**LEMON FROSTING**
- 1 container (16 ounces) DUNCAN HINES® Vanilla Frosting
- 1 teaspoon grated lemon peel
- ¼ teaspoon lemon extract
- 3 to 4 drops yellow food coloring
- Yellow and orange gumdrops, for garnish

**1.** Preheat oven to 350°F. Place 30 (2½-inch) paper liners in muffin cups.

**2. For cupcakes,** combine cake mix, eggs, water, oil and poppy seed in large bowl. Beat at medium speed of electric mixer 2 minutes. Fill paper liners about half full. Bake 18 to 21 minutes or until toothpick inserted in center comes out clean. Cool in pans 5 minutes. Remove to cooling racks. Cool completely.

**3. For Lemon Frosting,** combine Vanilla frosting, lemon peel and lemon extract in small bowl. Tint with yellow food coloring to desired color. Frost cupcakes with lemon frosting. Decorate with gumdrops.

*Makes 30 cupcakes*

## tip

To make cutting the gumdrops easier, dip your knife in sugar between each cut to help prevent the gumdrop from sticking to the knife.

Lemon Poppy Seed Cupcakes

# Polka Dot Cupcakes

**Topping**
- ½ cup (4 ounces) cream cheese, softened
- 1 egg
- 2 tablespoons granulated sugar
- ⅔ cup NESTLÉ® TOLL HOUSE Semi-Sweet Chocolate Mini Morsels

**Cupcakes**
- 1 package (16 ounces) pound cake mix
- 1 cup LIBBY'S® Solid Pack Pumpkin
- ⅓ cup water
- 2 eggs
- 2 teaspoons pumpkin pie spice
- 1 teaspoon baking soda

**FOR TOPPING**
**BEAT** cream cheese, egg and granulated sugar in small mixer bowl until smooth. Stir in morsels.

**FOR CUPCAKES**
**COMBINE** cake mix, pumpkin, water, eggs, pumpkin pie spice and baking soda in large mixer bowl; beat on medium speed for 3 minutes. Pour batter into paper-lined muffin cups, filling ¾ full. Spoon about 1 tablespoon topping over batter.

**BAKE** in preheated 325°F. oven for 25 to 30 minutes or until wooden pick inserted in center comes out clean. Cool in pans on wire racks for 10 minutes. Remove to wire racks to cool completely.

*Makes 16 cupcakes*

# Honey Chocolate Chip Cupcakes

- ½ cup butter or margarine, softened
- ⅔ cup honey
- 1 egg
- ½ teaspoon vanilla extract
- 1¼ cups all-purpose flour
- ½ teaspoon salt
- ½ teaspoon baking soda

**Topping**
- ⅓ cup honey
- 1 egg
- ½ teaspoon vanilla extract
- ⅛ teaspoon salt
- 1 cup semi-sweet chocolate chips
- ½ cup chopped walnuts

Using electric mixer, beat butter until light; gradually add honey, beating until light and creamy. Beat in egg and vanilla.

In medium bowl, combine flour, salt and baking soda; gradually add to butter mixture, mixing until blended. Spoon batter into

16 paper-lined or greased 2½-inch muffin cups. Bake at 350°F for 10 minutes.

Meanwhile, prepare topping. Using electric mixture, beat honey, egg, vanilla and salt until light; stir in chocolate chips and nuts. Remove cupcakes from oven. Spoon 1 tablespoon topping over each partially-baked cupcake. Return to oven; bake at 350°F for additional 12 to 15 minutes or until topping is set. Cool in pans on wire racks. *Makes 16 cupcakes*

*Favorite recipe from* **National Honey Board**

Warm nuts are easier to chop than cold or room temperature nuts. Place 1 cup of shelled nuts in a microwavable dish and heat at HIGH about 30 seconds or just until warm; chop as desired.

# Double Chocolate Cocoa Cupcakes

¾ **cup shortening**
1¼ **cups granulated sugar**
2 **eggs**
1 **teaspoon vanilla extract**
1¾ **cups all-purpose flour**
½ **cup HERSHEY'S Cocoa**
1 **teaspoon baking soda**
½ **teaspoon salt**
1 **cup milk**
1 **cup HERSHEY'S MINI CHIPS™ Semi-Sweet Chocolate**
**Powdered sugar**

**1.** Heat oven to 375°F. Line muffin cups (2½ inches in diameter) with paper bake cups.

**2.** Beat shortening and granulated sugar in large bowl until fluffy. Add eggs and vanilla; beat well. Stir together flour, cocoa, baking soda and salt; add alternately with milk to shortening mixture, beating well after each addition. Stir in mini chips. Fill prepared muffin cups about ¾ full with batter.

**3.** Bake 20 to 25 minutes or until cupcake springs back when touched lightly in center. Remove from pans to wire racks. Cool completely. Sift powdered sugar over tops of cupcakes.
*Makes about 2 dozen cupcakes*

## Red's® Rockin' Rainbow Cupcakes

2¼ cups all-purpose flour
1 tablespoon baking powder
½ teaspoon salt
1⅔ cups granulated sugar
½ cup (1 stick) butter, softened
1 cup milk
2 teaspoons vanilla extract
3 large egg whites
    Blue and assorted food
    colorings
1 container (16 ounces) white
    frosting
1½ cups "M&M's"® Chocolate
    Mini Baking Bits, divided

Preheat oven to 350°F. Lightly grease 24 (2¾-inch) muffin cups or line with paper or foil liners; set aside. In large bowl combine flour, baking powder and salt. Blend in sugar, butter, milk and vanilla; beat about 2 minutes. Add egg whites; beat 2 minutes. Divide batter evenly among prepared muffin cups. Place 2 drops desired food coloring into each muffin cup. Swirl gently with knife. Sprinkle evenly with ¾ cup "M&M's"® Chocolate Mini Baking Bits. Bake 20 to 25 minutes or until toothpick inserted in center comes out clean. Cool completely on wire racks. Combine frosting and blue food coloring. Spread frosting over cupcakes; decorate with remaining ¾ cup "M&M's"® Chocolate Mini Baking Bits to make rainbows. Store in tightly covered container.

*Makes 24 cupcakes*

## Quick Pumpkin Cupcakes

1 package (16 ounces) pound
    cake mix
2 eggs
1 cup LIBBY'S® Solid Pack
    Pumpkin
⅓ cup water
2 teaspoons pumpkin pie spice
1 teaspoon baking soda
    Prepared vanilla frosting

COMBINE all ingredients except frosting in large mixer bowl; beat on medium speed for 3 minutes. Pour batter into paper-lined muffin cups, filling ¾ full.

BAKE in preheated 325°F. oven for 25 to 30 minutes or until wooden pick inserted in center comes out clean. Cool in pan on wire rack for 10 minutes. Remove to wire rack to cool completely. Spread with frosting.

*Makes 14 cupcakes*

Red's® Rockin' Rainbow Cupcakes

# Mini Turtle Cupcakes

- 1 package (21.5 ounces) brownie mix plus ingredients to prepare mix
- ½ cup chopped pecans
- 1 cup prepared or home-made dark chocolate frosting
- ½ cup chopped pecans, toasted
- 12 caramels, unwrapped
- 1 to 2 tablespoons whipping cream

**1.** Heat oven to 350°F. Line 54 mini (1½-inch) muffin cups with paper muffin cup liners.

**2.** Prepare brownie batter as directed on package. Stir in chopped pecans.

**3.** Spoon batter into prepared muffin cups filling ⅔ full. Bake 18 minutes or until toothpick inserted into centers comes out clean. Cool in pans on wire racks 5 minutes. Remove cupcakes to racks; cool completely. (At this point, cupcakes may be frozen up to 3 months. Thaw at room temperature before frosting.)

**4.** Spread frosting over cooled cupcakes; top with pecans.

**5.** Combine caramels and 1 tablespoon cream in small saucepan. Cook over low heat until caramels are melted and mixture is smooth, stirring constantly. Add additional 1 tablespoon cream if needed. Drizzle caramel decoratively over cupcakes. Store at room temperature up to 24 hours or cover and refrigerate for up to 3 days before serving.

*Makes 54 mini cupcakes*

## tip

To toast nuts, spread in a single layer on a baking sheet and toast in a preheated 350oF oven for 8 to 10 minutes or until very lightly browned.

Mini Turtle Cupcakes

# Campbell's® Healthy Request® Glazed Carrot Raisin Cupcakes

- 1 **package spice cake mix (about 18 ounces)**
- 1 **can (10¾ ounces) CAMPBELL'S® HEALTHY REQUEST® Condensed Tomato Soup**
- ½ **cup water**
- 2 **eggs**
- 1 **medium carrot, shredded (about ½ cup)**
- ½ **cup raisins**
- 1 **cup confectioners' sugar**
- 3 **tablespoons unsweetened apple juice**

**1.** Preheat oven to 350°F. Place liners in 24 (2½-inch) muffin-pan cups. Set aside.

**2.** Mix cake mix, soup, water and eggs according to package directions. Fold in carrot and raisins. Spoon batter into cups, filling almost full.

**3.** Bake 20 minutes or until toothpick inserted in center comes out clean. Remove from pan and cool completely on wire rack.

**4.** Mix sugar and juice until smooth. Frost cupcakes.

*Makes 24 cupcakes*

**Prep Time:** 10 minutes
**Cook Time:** 20 minutes
**Cool Time:** 20 minutes

Fresh carrots can be shredded easily by using the large holes of a four-sided grater or with a food processor fitted with the shredding disc.

Campbell's® Healthy Request®
Glazed Carrot Raisin Cupcakes

## Miniature Cheesecakes

• • • • • • • • • • • • • • • • • • • • • • • • • • • • • • • • • •

    1  **package (11.1 ounces) JELL-O® No Bake Real Cheesecake**
    2  **tablespoons sugar**
    ⅓  **cup butter or margarine, melted**
 1½  **cups cold milk**
    2  **squares BAKER'S® Semi-Sweet Baking Chocolate, melted (optional)**

**MIX** crumbs from mix, sugar and butter thoroughly with fork in medium bowl until crumbs are well moistened. Press onto bottoms of 12 paper-lined or foil-lined muffin cups.

**BEAT** milk and filling mix with electric mixer on low speed until blended. Beat on medium speed 3 minutes. (Filling will be thick.) Spoon over crumb mixture in muffin cups. Drizzle with melted chocolate, if desired.

**REFRIGERATE** at least 1 hour or until ready to serve. Garnish as desired. *Makes 12 servings*

**Preparation Time:** 15 minutes
**Refrigerating Time:** 1 hour

Miniature Cheesecakes

# Cappuccino Cupcakes

- **1 package (18.25 ounces) dark chocolate cake mix**
- **1⅓ cups decaffeinated brewed or instant coffee at room temperature**
- **⅓ cup vegetable oil or melted butter**
- **3 large eggs**
- **1 container (16 ounces) prepared vanilla frosting**
- **2 tablespoons coffee liqueur or water**
- **Grated chocolate***
- **Chocolate-covered coffee beans (optional)**
- **Additional coffee liqueur (optional)**

*Grate half of a 3- or 4-ounce milk chocolate, dark chocolate or espresso chocolate candy bar on the large holes of a standing grater.*

**1.** Preheat oven to 350°F. Line 24 regular-size (2½-inch) muffin cups with paper muffin cup liners.

**2.** Beat cake mix, coffee, oil and eggs with electric mixer at low speed 30 seconds. Beat at medium speed 2 minutes.

**3.** Spoon batter into prepared muffin cups filling ⅔ full. Bake 18 to 20 minutes or until toothpick inserted in centers comes out clean. Cool in pans on wire racks 10 minutes. Remove cupcakes to racks; cool completely. (At this point, cupcakes may be frozen up to 3 months. Thaw at room temperature before frosting.)

**4.** Combine frosting and 2 tablespoons liqueur in small bowl; mix well. Before frosting, poke about 10 holes in cupcake with toothpick. Pour 1 to 2 teaspoons liqueur over top of each cupcake, if desired. Frost and sprinkle with chocolate. Garnish with chocolate-covered coffee beans, if desired.

*Makes 24 cupcakes*

## tip

When brewing coffee, always be sure to use cold water. If tap water has a mineral taste it may adversely affect the coffee flavor. Use bottled water instead.

Cappuccino Cupcakes

# Banana Split Cupcakes

- 1 (18.25 ounces) yellow cake mix, divided
- 1 cup water
- 1 cup mashed ripe bananas
- 3 eggs
- 1 cup chopped drained maraschino cherries
- 1½ cups miniature semi-sweet chocolate chips, divided
- 1½ cups prepared vanilla frosting
- 1 cup marshmallow creme
- 1 teaspoon shortening
- 30 whole maraschino cherries, drained and patted dry

**1.** Preheat oven to 350°F. Line 30 regular-size (2½-inch) muffin cups with paper muffin cup liners.

**2.** Reserve 2 tablespoons cake mix. Combine remaining cake mix, water, bananas and eggs in large bowl. Beat at low speed of electric mixer until moistened, about 30 seconds. Beat at medium speed 2 minutes. Combine chopped cherries and reserved cake mix in small bowl. Stir chopped cherry mixture and 1 cup chocolate chips into batter.

**3.** Spoon batter into prepared muffin cups. Bake 15 to 20 minutes or until toothpick inserted in centers comes out clean. Cool in pans on wire racks 10 minutes. Remove to wire racks; cool completely.

**4.** Combine frosting and marshmallow creme in medium bowl until well blended. Frost each cupcake with frosting mixture.

**5.** Combine remaining ½ cup chocolate chips and shortening in small microwavable bowl. Microwave at HIGH 30 to 45 seconds, stirring after 30 seconds, or until smooth. Drizzle chocolate mixture over cupcakes. Place one whole cherry on each cupcake.

*Makes 30 cupcakes*

**Note:** If desired, top cupcakes with colored sprinkles.

Banana Split Cupcakes

# Chocolate Tiramisu Cupcakes

**Cupcakes**

    1 **package (18.25 ounces) chocolate cake mix**
    2 **tablespoons instant espresso powder**
  1¼ **cups water**
    3 **large eggs**
   ⅓ **cup vegetable oil or melted butter**
    2 **tablespoons brandy (optional)**

**Frosting**

    8 **ounces mascarpone cheese or cream cheese**
 1½ **to 1¾ cups powdered sugar**
    2 **tablespoons coffee-flavored liqueur**
    1 **tablespoon unsweetened cocoa powder**

**1.** Preheat oven to 350°F. Line 30 regular-size (2½-inch) muffin cups with paper muffin cup liners.

**2.** Beat all cupcake ingredients with electric mixer at low speed 30 seconds. Beat at medium speed 2 minutes.

**3.** Spoon batter into prepared cups filling ⅔ full. Bake 20 to 22 minutes or until toothpick inserted in centers comes out clean. Cool in pans on wire racks 10 minutes. Remove cupcakes to racks; cool completely.

(At this point, cupcakes may be frozen up to 3 months. Thaw at room temperature before frosting.)

**4.** For frosting, beat mascarpone cheese and 1½ cups powdered sugar with electric mixer at medium speed until well blended. Add liqueur; beat until well blended. If frosting is too soft, beat in additional powdered sugar or chill until spreadable.

**5.** Frost cooled cupcakes with frosting. Place cocoa in strainer; shake over cupcakes. Store at room temperature up to 24 hours or cover and refrigerate for up to 3 days before serving.

*Makes 30 cupcakes*

Mascarpone cheese hails from Italy's Lombardy region. It is an ivory-colored, soft, delicate cheese that is traditionally used in classic Tiramisu.

Chocolate Tiramisu Cupcakes

# Caramel Apple Cupcakes

1 package butter-recipe yellow cake mix plus ingredients to prepare
1 cup chopped dried apples
Caramel Frosting (recipe follows)
Chopped nuts (optional)

**1.** Preheat oven to 375°F. Line 24 regular-size (2½-inch) muffin pan cups with paper muffin cup liners.

**2.** Prepare cake mix according to package directions. Stir in apples. Spoon batter into prepared muffin pans.

**3.** Bake 15 to 20 minutes or until toothpick inserted into centers comes out clean. Cool in pans on wire racks 10 minutes. Remove to racks; cool completely.

**4.** Prepare Caramel Frosting. Frost cupcakes. Sprinkle cupcakes with nuts, if desired.

*Makes 24 cupcakes*

## Caramel Frosting

3 tablespoons butter
1 cup packed brown sugar
½ cup evaporated milk
⅛ teaspoon salt
3¾ cups powdered sugar
¾ teaspoon vanilla

**1.** Melt butter in 2-quart saucepan. Stir in brown sugar, evaporated milk and salt. Bring to a boil, stirring constantly. Remove from heat; cool to lukewarm.

**2.** Beat in powdered sugar until frosting is of spreading consistency. Blend in vanilla.

## tip

To keep the dried apples from sticking to the knife while chopping them, spray the knife with nonstick cooking spray before you begin.

# Peanut Butter Surprise

- 2 cups all-purpose flour
- 2 teaspoons baking powder
- ¼ teaspoon salt
- 1¾ cups sugar
- ½ cup (1 stick) butter, softened
- ¾ cup 2% or whole milk
- 1 teaspoon vanilla
- 3 large egg whites
- 2 (3-ounce) bittersweet chocolate candy bars, melted and cooled
- 30 mini peanut butter cups
- 1 container prepared chocolate frosting
- 3 ounces white chocolate candy bar, broken into chunks

**1.** Preheat oven to 350°F. Line 30 regular-size (2½-inch) muffin cups with paper muffin cup liners.

**2.** For cupcakes, combine flour, baking powder and salt in medium bowl; mix well and set aside. Beat sugar and butter with electric mixer at medium speed 1 minute. Add milk and vanilla. Beat with electric mixer at low speed 30 seconds. Gradually beat in flour mixture; beat at medium speed 2 minutes. Add egg whites; beat 1 minute. Stir in melted chocolate.

**3.** Spoon 1 heaping tablespoon batter into each prepared muffin cup; use back of spoon to slightly spread batter over bottom. Place one mini peanut butter cup in center of each cupcake. Spoon 1 heaping tablespoon batter over peanut butter cup; use back of spoon to smooth out batter. (Do not fill cups more than ¾ full.)

**4.** Bake 24 to 26 minutes or until puffed and golden brown. Cool in pans on wire racks 10 minutes. (Center of cupcakes will sink slightly upon cooling.) Remove cupcakes to racks; cool completely. (At this point, cupcakes may be frozen up to 3 months.) Spread frosting over cooled cupcakes.

**5.** For white drizzle, place white chocolate in small resealable freezer bag. Microwave at HIGH 30 to 40 seconds. Turn bag over; microwave additional 30 seconds or until chocolate is melted. Cut off tiny corner of bag; pipe chocolate decoratively over frosted cupcakes. Store at room temperature up to 24 hours or cover and refrigerate up to 3 days before serving.

*Makes 30 cupcakes*

# Vanilla-Strawberry Cupcakes

**Cupcakes**
- 2 cups all-purpose flour
- 2 teaspoons baking powder
- ¼ teaspoon salt
- 1¾ cups granulated sugar
- ½ cup (1 stick) butter, softened
- ¾ cup 2% or whole milk
- 1½ teaspoons vanilla
- 3 large egg whites
- ½ cup strawberry preserves

**Frosting**
- 1 package (8 ounces) cream cheese (do not use fat-free), chilled and cut into cubes
- 4 tablespoons butter, softened
- 2 teaspoons vanilla
- 2 cups powdered sugar
- 1 to 1½ cups small fresh strawberry slices

**1.** Preheat oven to 350°F. Line 28 regular-size (2½-inch) muffin pan cups with paper muffin cup liners.

**2.** For cupcakes, combine flour, baking powder and salt in medium bowl; mix well and set aside. Beat granulated sugar and butter with electric mixer at medium speed 1 minute. Add milk and vanilla. Beat at low speed 30 seconds. Gradually beat in flour mixture; beat at medium speed 2 minutes. Add egg whites; beat 1 minute.

**3.** Spoon batter into prepared muffin cups filling ½ full. Drop 1 teaspoon preserves on top of batter; swirl into batter with toothpick. Bake 20 to 22 minutes or until toothpick inserted into centers comes out clean. Cool in pans on wire racks 10 minutes. Remove cupcakes to racks; cool completely. (At this point, cupcakes may be frozen up to 3 months. Thaw at room temperature before frosting.)

**4.** For frosting, process cream cheese, butter and vanilla in food processor or just until combined. Add powdered sugar; pulse just until sugar is incorporated. (Do not overmix or frosting will be too soft to spread.)

**5.** Spread frosting over cooled cupcakes; decorate with sliced strawberries. Serve within 1 hour or refrigerate up to 8 hours before serving.

*Makes 28 cupcakes*

# Berry Surprise Cupcakes

* * * * * * * * * * * * * * * *

1 package DUNCAN HINES® Moist Deluxe® White Cake Mix

3 egg whites

1⅓ cups water

2 tablespoons vegetable oil

3 sheets (0.5 ounce each) strawberry chewy fruit snacks

1 container DUNCAN HINES® Vanilla Frosting

2 pouches (0.9 ounce each) chewy fruit snack shapes, for garnish (optional)

**1.** Preheat oven to 350°F. Place 24 (2½-inch) paper liners in muffin cups.

**2.** Combine cake mix, egg whites, water and oil in large bowl. Beat at low speed with electric mixer until moistened. Beat at medium speed 2 minutes. Fill each liner half full with batter.

**3.** Cut three fruit snack sheets into 9 equal pieces. (You will have 3 extra squares.) Place each fruit snack piece on top of batter in each cup. Pour remaining batter equally over each. Bake at 350°F 18 to 23 minutes or until toothpick inserted in center comes out clean. Cool in pans 5 minutes. Remove to cooling racks. Cool completely. Frost cupcakes with Vanilla frosting. Decorate with fruit snack shapes, if desired.

*Makes 12 to 16 servings*

**Tip:** To make a Berry Surprise Cake, prepare cake following package directions. Pour half the batter into prepared 13×9×2-inch pan. Place 4 fruit snack sheets evenly on top. Pour remaining batter over all. Bake and cool as directed on package. Frost and decorate as described above.

## *tip*

To give these cupcakes a festive touch any time of year, simply use holiday print or colored paper liners.

**Berry Surprise Cupcakes**

# Black Bottom Cheesecake Cups

**CHEESECAKE FILLING**
- 1 container (8 ounces) fat-free cream cheese
- ¼ cup sugar
- 1 egg

**CHOCOLATE BATTER**
- 1½ cups all-purpose flour
- ¾ cup sugar
- ⅓ cup unsweetened cocoa powder
- 1 teaspoon baking soda
- ½ teaspoon salt
- 1 cup water
- ⅓ cup Dried Plum Purée (recipe follows) or prepared dried plum butter or 1 jar (2½ ounces) first-stage baby food dried plums
- 1 tablespoon instant espresso coffee powder *or* 2 tablespoons instant coffee granules
- 1 tablespoon white vinegar
- 2 teaspoons vanilla
- ½ cup semisweet chocolate chips

**ALMOND TOPPING**
- ¼ cup finely chopped blanched almonds
- 2 tablespoons sugar

Preheat oven to 350°F. Line eighteen 2¾-inch (⅓-cup capacity) muffin cups with cupcake liners. Coat liners lightly with vegetable cooking spray. To make filling, in small mixer bowl, beat filling ingredients at medium speed until smooth; set aside.

To make chocolate batter, in large bowl, combine first five batter ingredients. In medium bowl, beat water, Dried Plum Purée, espresso powder, vinegar and vanilla until blended. Mix into flour mixture. Spoon into muffin cups, dividing equally. Top each with heaping teaspoonful of filling mixture. Sprinkle with chocolate chips.

To make topping, mix almonds and sugar; sprinkle over chocolate chips. Bake in center of oven about 25 minutes or until pick inserted into chocolate portion comes out clean. Cool in pans 5 minutes; remove from pans to wire racks to cool completely.

*Makes 18 cupcakes*

**Dried Plum Purée:** Combine 1⅓ cups (8 ounces) pitted dried plums and 6 tablespoons hot water in container of food processor or blender. Pulse on and off until dried plums are finely chopped and smooth. Store leftovers in a covered container in the refrigerator for up to two months. Makes 1 cup.

*Favorite recipe from **California Dried Plum Board***

# Chocolate Peanut Butter Cups

• • • • • • • • • • • • • • •

1 package DUNCAN HINES®
Moist Deluxe® Swiss
Chocolate Cake Mix
1 container DUNCAN HINES®
Vanilla Frosting
½ cup creamy peanut butter
15 miniature peanut butter cup
candies, wrappers
removed, cut in half
vertically

**1.** Preheat oven to 350°F. Place
30 (2½-inch) paper liners in
muffin cups.

**2.** Prepare, bake and cool
cupcakes following package
directions for basic recipe.

**3.** Combine Vanilla frosting and
peanut butter in medium bowl.
Stir until smooth. Frost one
cupcake. Decorate with peanut
butter cup candy, cut-side down.
Repeat with remaining cupcakes.
*Makes 30 servings*

**Tip:** You may substitute
DUNCAN HINES® Moist Deluxe®
Devil's Food, Dark Chocolate
Fudge or Butter Recipe Fudge
Cake Mix flavors for Swiss
Chocolate Cake Mix.

# Cherry Cupcakes

• • • • • • • • • • • • • • •

1 (18¾-ounce) box chocolate
cake mix
3 eggs
1⅓ cups water
½ cup vegetable oil
1 (21-ounce) can cherry pie
filling
1 (16-ounce) can vanilla
frosting

Prepare cake mix according to
package directions, adding eggs,
water and oil. Pour batter into
24 paper-lined muffin-pan cups,
filling two-thirds full.

Remove 24 cherries from cherry
filling; set aside. Spoon a
generous teaspoon of remaining
cherry filling onto the center of
each cupcake.

Bake in preheated 350°F oven
20 to 25 minutes. Cool in pans
on wire racks 10 minutes.
Remove from pan. Let cool
completely. Frost cupcakes with
vanilla frosting. Garnish
cupcakes with reserved cherries.
*Makes 24 cupcakes*

*Favorite recipe from **Cherry
Marketing Institute***

Chocolate Peanut Butter Cups

# Party Time

## Ice Cream Cone Cupcakes

• • • • • • • • • • • • • • • • • • • • • • • • • • • • • • • • • • • •

1 package (18¼ ounces) white cake mix plus ingredients to prepare

2 tablespoons nonpareils*

2 packages (1¾ ounces each) flat-bottomed ice cream cones (about 24 cones)

1 container (16 ounces) vanilla or chocolate frosting
Candies and other decorations

*Nonpareils are tiny, round, brightly colored sprinkles used for cake and cookie decorating.*

**1.** Preheat oven to 350°F. Prepare cake mix according to package directions. Stir in nonpareils.

**2.** Spoon ¼ cup batter into each ice cream cone.

**3.** Stand cones on cookie sheet. Bake cones until toothpick inserted into center of cake comes out clean, about 20 minutes. Cool on wire racks. Frost each filled cone. Decorate as desired.

*Makes 24 cupcakes*

**Note:** Cupcakes are best served the day they are prepared. Store loosely covered.

Ice Cream Cone Cupcakes

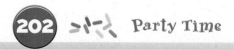

# Frizzy the Clown Cupcakes

• • • • • • • • • • • • • • • • • •

24 **Reynolds® Bake Cups**
1 **package (about 18 ounces) cake mix**
1 **container (16 ounces) vanilla frosting**
   **Orange food coloring**
   **Powdered sugar**
12 **gummy fruit-flavored ring candies**
24 **small gumdrops**
48 **mini candy coated plain chocolate candies**
   **Red string licorice**

**PREHEAT** oven to 350°F. Place Reynolds Bake Cups in muffin pans; set aside. Prepare cake mix following package directions for 24 cupcakes. Spoon batter into bake cups. Bake as directed. Cool.

**FROST** cupcakes; set aside.

**TINT** a small amount of frosting with orange food coloring for Frizzy's hair. Add powdered sugar to frosting until it is no longer sticky (has consistency of cookie dough). Press frosting through garlic press or fine strainer. Pinch strands of frosting together and press on cupcake. For mouth, cut a section of a gummy fruit-flavored ring candy, add to cupcake. Add gumdrop for the nose, chocolate candies for eyes and red string licorice for eyebrows.

*Makes 24 cupcakes*

# Beehives

• • • • • • • • • • • • • • • • • •

1 **tub (8 ounces) COOL WHIP® Whipped Topping, thawed**
8 **cupcakes**
   **Yellow jelly beans**
   **Chocolate decorating gel**
   **Black string licorice**

**SPOON** whipped topping into large zipper-style storage bag. Close bag tightly, squeezing out excess air. Fold down top tightly; snip small piece (about ½ inch) off 1 corner.

**HOLDING** top of bag tightly, pipe whipped topping onto each cupcake to resemble beehives. Make stripes on jelly beans with decorating gel to resemble bumblebees; place on whipped topping. Add string licorice to form antennae. Serve immediately. Store leftover cupcakes in refrigerator.

*Makes 8 servings*

Frizzy the Clown Cupcakes

# "Go Fly a Kite" Cupcakes

· · · · · · · · · · · · · · · · · · · · · · · · ·

1²/₃ cups all-purpose flour
½ cup unsweetened cocoa
    powder
1 teaspoon baking powder
½ teaspoon baking soda
¼ teaspoon salt
1¾ cups granulated sugar
¼ cup firmly packed light
    brown sugar
½ cup vegetable shortening
1 cup buttermilk
3 large eggs
2 tablespoons vegetable oil
¾ teaspoon vanilla extract
1½ cups "M&M's"® Chocolate
    Mini Baking Bits, divided
24 graham cracker squares
1 container (16 ounces) white
    frosting
    Assorted food colorings

Preheat oven to 350°F. Lightly grease 24 (2¾-inch) muffin cups or line with foil or paper liners; set aside. In large bowl combine flour, cocoa powder, baking powder, baking soda and salt; stir in sugars. Beat in shortening until well combined. Beat in buttermilk, eggs, oil and vanilla. Divide batter among prepared muffin cups. Sprinkle 1 teaspoon "M&M's"® Chocolate Mini Baking Bits over batter in each muffin cup. Bake 20 to 25 minutes or until toothpick

inserted in centers comes out clean. Cool completely on wire racks. Using serrated knife and back and forth sawing motion, gently cut graham crackers into kite shapes. (Do not press down on cracker while cutting.) Reserve 1 cup frosting. Tint remaining frosting desired color. Frost graham crackers and decorate with "M&M's"® Chocolate Mini Baking Bits. Tint reserved frosting sky blue; frost cupcakes. Place small blob frosting at one edge of cupcake; stand kites in frosting on cupcakes. Make kite tails with "M&M's"® Chocolate Mini Baking Bits. Store in tightly covered container.

*Makes 24 cupcakes*

### tip

To make sky-blue colored frosting, begin by adding one drop of blue food coloring to remaining 1 cup frosting. Add an additional drop if a darker blue is desired.

"Go Fly a Kite" Cupcakes

# Play Ball

- - - - - - - - - - - - - - - - - -

2 cups plus 1 tablespoon
   all-purpose flour
¾ cup granulated sugar
¾ cup packed brown sugar
1 tablespoon baking powder
1 teaspoon salt
½ teaspoon baking soda
½ cup shortening
1¼ cups milk
3 eggs
1½ teaspoons vanilla
½ cup mini semisweet
   chocolate chips
1 container (16 ounces) vanilla
   frosting
   Assorted candies and food
   colorings

**1.** Preheat oven to 350°F. Line 24 regular-size (2½-inch) muffin cups with paper muffin cup liners.

**2.** Combine 2 cups flour, sugars, baking powder, salt and baking soda in medium bowl. Beat shortening, milk, eggs and vanilla with electric mixer at medium speed until well combined. Add dry ingredients; blend well. Beat at high speed 3 minutes, scraping side of bowl frequently. Toss mini chocolate chips with 1 tablespoon flour; stir into batter. Divide evenly between prepared muffin cups.

**3.** Bake 20 minutes or until toothpick inserted into center comes out clean. Cool in pan on wire racks 5 minutes. Remove cupcakes to racks; cool completely. Decorate with desired frostings and candies as shown in photo.

*Makes 24 cupcakes*

## tip

It's all about sports. These cupcakes are the perfect treats to celebrate the big game. Decorate the cupcakes like the sports ball desired.

Play Ball

# Mini Cocoa Cupcake Kabobs

1 cup sugar
1 cup all-purpose flour
⅓ cup HERSHEY'S Cocoa
¾ teaspoon baking powder
¾ teaspoon baking soda
½ teaspoon salt
1 egg
½ cup milk
¼ cup vegetable oil
1 teaspoon vanilla extract
½ cup boiling water
 Lickety-Split Cocoa Frosting
  (recipe follows)
 Jelly beans or sugar
  nonpareils and/or
  decorating frosting
 Marshmallows
 Strawberries
 Wooden skewers

**1.** Heat oven to 350°F. Spray small muffin cups (1¾ inches in diameter) with vegetable cooking spray.

**2.** Stir together sugar, flour, cocoa, baking powder, baking soda and salt in medium bowl. Add egg, milk, oil and vanilla; beat on medium speed of mixer 2 minutes. Stir in boiling water (batter will be thin). Fill muffin cups about ⅔ full with batter.

**3.** Bake 10 minutes or until wooden pick inserted in center comes out clean. Cool slightly; remove from pans to wire racks. Cool completely. Frost with Lickety-Split Cocoa Frosting. Garnish with jelly beans, nonpariels and/or white frosting piped onto cupcake. Alternate cupcakes, marshmallows and strawberries on skewers.
*Makes about 4 dozen cupcakes*

**Lickety-Split Cocoa Frosting:** Beat 3 tablespoons softened butter or margarine in small bowl until creamy. Add 1¼ cups powdered sugar, ¼ cup HERSHEY'S Cocoa, 2 to 3 tablespoons milk and ½ teaspoon vanilla extract until smooth and of desired consistency. Makes about 1 cup frosting.

**Note:** Number of kabobs will be determined by length of skewer used and number of cupcakes, marshmallows and strawberries placed on each skewer.

Mini Cocoa Cupcake Kabobs

# Captivating Caterpillar Cupcakes

1 package DUNCAN HINES®
   Moist Deluxe® White Cake
   Mix
3 egg whites
1⅓ cups water
2 tablespoons vegetable oil
½ cup star decors, divided
1 container DUNCAN HINES®
   Vanilla Frosting
   Green food coloring
6 chocolate sandwich cookies,
   finely crushed (see Tip)
½ cup candy-coated chocolate
   pieces
⅓ cup assorted jelly beans
   Assorted nonpareil decors

**1.** Preheat oven to 350°F. Place 24 (2½-inch) paper liners in muffin cups.

**2.** Combine cake mix, egg whites, water and oil in large bowl. Beat at low speed with electric mixer until moistened. Beat at medium speed 2 minutes. Fold in ⅓ cup star decors. Fill paper liners about half full. Bake at 350°F 18 to 23 minutes or until toothpick inserted in center comes out clean. Cool in pans 5 minutes. Remove to cooling racks. Cool completely.

**3.** Tint Vanilla frosting with green food coloring. Frost one cupcake. Sprinkle ½ teaspoon chocolate cookie crumbs on frosting. Arrange 4 candy-coated chocolate pieces to form caterpillar body. Place jelly bean at one end to form head. Attach remaining star and nonpareil decors with dots of frosting to form eyes. Repeat with remaining cupcakes.

*Makes 24 cupcakes*

To finely crush chocolate sandwich cookies, place cookies in resealable plastic bag. Remove excess air from bag; seal. Press rolling pin on top of cookies to break into pieces. Continue pressing until evenly crushed.

Captivating Caterpillar
Cupcakes

# Banana Split Cups

**1 package (18 ounces) refrigerated chocolate chip cookie dough**

**⅔ cup "M&M's"® Chocolate Mini Baking Bits, divided**

**1 ripe medium banana, cut into 18 slices and halved**

**¾ cup chocolate syrup, divided**

**2¼ cups any flavor ice cream, softened**

**Aerosol whipped topping**

**¼ cup chopped maraschino cherries**

Lightly grease 36 (1¾-inch) mini muffin cups. Cut dough into 36 equal pieces; roll into balls. Place 1 ball in bottom of each muffin cup. Press dough onto bottoms and up sides of muffin cups; chill 15 minutes. Press ⅓ cup "M&M's"® Chocolate Mini Baking Bits into bottoms and sides of dough cups. Preheat oven to 350°F. Bake cookies 8 to 9 minutes. Cookies will be puffy. Remove from oven; gently press down center of each cookie. Return to oven 1 minute. Cool cookies in muffin cups 5 minutes. Remove to wire racks; cool completely. Place 1 banana half slice in each cookie cup; top with ½ teaspoon chocolate syrup. Place about ½ teaspoon "M&M's"® Chocolate Mini Baking Bits in each cookie cup; top with 1 tablespoon ice cream. Top each cookie cup with ½ teaspoon chocolate syrup, whipped topping, remaining "M&M's"® Chocolate Mini Baking Bits and 1 maraschino cherry piece. Store covered in freezer.

*Makes 3 dozen cookies*

### tip

To soften ice cream, place a 1-quart container of hard-packed ice cream in the microwave and heat at MEDIUM (50% power) about 20 seconds or just until softened.

**Banana Split Cups**

# All-American Ice Cream Cups

- 18 Reynolds® Foil Bake Cups
- 2 cups loosely packed coconut macaroon cookie crumbs (10 cookies, 2 inches diameter)
- ¼ cup apricot preserves
- ½ teaspoon almond extract
- ½ gallon vanilla ice cream, slightly softened
- 18 maraschino cherries
- ½ cup sliced almonds
  Reynolds Wrap® Heavy Duty Aluminum Foil

**PLACE** Reynolds Foil Bake Cups in muffin pans; set aside.

**COMBINE** cookie crumbs, apricot preserves and almond extract. Stir with fork until crumbs are coated. Press one rounded tablespoon crumb mixture in bottom of each bake cup. Working quickly, spoon one scoop of ice cream into each bake cup. Top each dessert with cherry and sliced almonds.

**FREEZE** until serving time. For freezer storage, cover with Reynolds Wrap Heavy Duty Aluminum Foil.

*Makes 18 desserts*

# Porcupine Cupcakes

- 1 package DUNCAN HINES® Moist Deluxe® Cake Mix (any flavor)
- 1 container DUNCAN HINES® Chocolate Frosting
  Sliced almonds

**1.** Preheat oven to 350°F. Place 2½-inch paper liners in 24 muffin cups.

**2.** Prepare, bake and cool cupcakes following package directions for basic recipe. Frost cupcakes with Chocolate frosting. Place sliced almonds upright on each cupcake to decorate as a "porcupine."
*Makes 24 cupcakes*

**Tip:** Slivered almonds can be used in place of sliced almonds.

All-American Ice Cream Cups

# Brownie Peanut Butter Cupcakes

- 18 Reynolds® Foil Bake Cups
- ⅓ cup creamy peanut butter
- ¼ cup light cream cheese
- 2 tablespoons sugar
- 1 egg
- 1 package (about 19 ounces) fudge brownie mix
- ½ cup candy coated peanut butter candies

**PREHEAT** oven to 350°F. Place Reynolds Foil Bake Cups in muffin pans or on cookie sheet; set aside. Beat peanut butter, cream cheese, sugar and egg in bowl, with electric mixer; set aside.

**PREPARE** brownie mix following package directions; set aside. Place 1 heaping teaspoon of peanut butter mixture in center of each bake cup. With spoon or small ice cream scoop, fill bake cups half full with brownie batter. Sprinkle each brownie cupcake with peanut butter candies.

**BAKE** 25 minutes, do not overbake. Cool.

*Makes 18 brownie cupcakes*

# Raindrop Cupcakes

- 1 package (2-layer size) white cake mix
- 1 package (4-serving size) JELL-O® Brand Berry Blue Flavor Gelatin
- 1 cup boiling water
- 1 tub (8 ounces) COOL WHIP® Whipped Topping, thawed
- Decorating gel
- Colored sugar (optional)

**HEAT** oven to 350°F.

**PREPARE** cake mix as directed on package, using egg whites. Spoon batter into paper-lined muffin pan, filling each cup ½ full. Bake as directed on package. Cool cupcakes in pan 15 minutes, then pierce with large fork at ¼-inch intervals.

**DISSOLVE** gelatin completely in boiling water in small bowl. Gradually spoon over cupcakes.

**REFRIGERATE** 3 to 4 hours. Frost with whipped topping. Draw umbrellas on cupcakes with decorating gel. Sprinkle with colored sugar. Store cupcakes in refrigerator.

*Makes 24 cupcakes*

Brownie Peanut Butter Cupcakes

## Snowman Cupcakes

- 1 **package (18.5 ounces) yellow or white cake mix plus ingredients to prepare mix**
- 2 **containers (16 ounces each) vanilla frosting**
- 4 **cups flaked coconut**
- 15 **large marshmallows**
- 15 **miniature chocolate covered peanut butter cups, unwrapped**
  **Small red candies and pretzel sticks for decoration**
  **Green and red decorating gel**

Preheat oven to 350°F. Line 15 regular-size (2½-inch) muffin pan cups and 15 small (about 1-inch) muffin pan cups with paper muffin cup liners. Prepare cake mix according to package directions. Spoon batter into muffin cups.

Bake 10 to 15 minutes for small cupcakes and 15 to 20 minutes for large cupcakes or until cupcakes are golden and toothpick inserted into centers comes out clean. Cool in pans on wire racks 10 minutes. Remove from pans to racks; cool completely. Remove paper liners.

*continued on page 222*

Snowman Cupcakes

**Snowman Cupcakes, continued**

For each snowman, frost bottom and side of 1 large cupcake; coat with coconut. Repeat with 1 small cupcake. Attach small cupcake to large cupcake with frosting to form snowman body. Attach marshmallow to small cupcake with frosting to form snowman head. Attach inverted peanut butter cup to marshmallow with frosting to form snowman hat. Use pretzels for arms and small red candies for buttons as shown in photo. Pipe faces with decorating gel as shown. Repeat with remaining cupcakes.

*Makes 15 snowmen*

For a change of pace, use licorice vines for the snowman's arms and chocolate chips or chocolate-covered coffee beans for his buttons.

# Valentine's Cupcakes

- **24 Reynolds® Valentine Bake Cups**
- **1 package (about 18 ounces) white cake mix**
- **1 container (16 ounces) white or pink frosting**
  **Red cinnamon candies**
  **Chocolate heart candies**
  **Cut-Rite® Wax Paper**

**PREHEAT** oven to 350°F. Place Reynolds Valentine Bake Cups in muffin pans; set aside. Prepare cake mix following package directions for 24 cupcakes. Spoon batter into bake cups. Bake as directed. Cool.

**FROST** cupcakes with white or pink frosting. Place red cinnamon candies around cupcake edges. Stand two chocolate heart candies in center of frosting or use a small cookie cutter to cut hearts from a chocolate candy bar. (To prevent chocolate candy bar from cracking, remove wrapper, place on a sheet of Cut-Rite Wax Paper and soften in microwave on DEFROST (30% power) 15 to 30 seconds.)

*Makes 24 cupcakes*

Valentine's Cupcakes

With Love

# Pretty in Pink Peppermint Cupcakes

- 1 package (18.25 ounces) white cake mix
- 1⅓ cups water
- 3 large egg whites
- 2 tablespoons vegetable oil or melted butter
- ½ teaspoon peppermint extract
- 3 to 4 drops red liquid food coloring *or* ¼ teaspoon gel food coloring
- 1 container (16 ounces) prepared vanilla frosting
- ½ cup crushed peppermint candies (about 16 candies)

**1.** Preheat oven to 350°F. Line 30 regular-size (2½-inch) muffin cups with pink or white paper muffin cup liners.

**2.** Beat cake mix, water, egg whites, oil, peppermint extract and food coloring with electric mixer at low speed 30 seconds. Beat at medium speed 2 minutes.

**3.** Spoon batter into prepared cups filling ¾ full. Bake 20 to 22 minutes or until toothpick inserted into center comes out clean. Cool in pans on wire racks 10 minutes. Remove cupcakes to racks; cool completely. (At this point, cupcakes may be frozen up to 3 months. Thaw at room temperature before frosting.)

**4.** Spread cooled cupcakes with frosting; top with crushed candies. Store at room temperature up to 24 hours or cover and refrigerate up to 3 days before serving.

*Makes about 30 cupcakes*

**tip**

To easily crush peppermint candies, place whole candies in resealable plastic food storage bags. Remove excess air from bag; seal. Press rolling pin firmly on top of candies to break into pieces.

Pretty in Pink Peppermint Cupcakes

# Edible Easter Baskets

. . . . . . . . . . . . . . . . . . . .

**1** package (about 18 ounces) refrigerated sugar cookie dough
**1** cup "M&M's"® Milk Chocolate Mini Baking Bits, divided
**1** teaspoon water
**1 to 2** drops green food coloring
**¾** cup sweetened shredded coconut
**¾** cup any flavor frosting
    Red licorice whips, cut into 3-inch lengths

Lightly grease 36 (1¾-inch) mini muffin cups. Cut dough into 36 equal pieces; roll into balls. Place 1 ball in each muffin cup. Press dough onto bottom and up side of each muffin cup; chill 15 minutes. Press ⅓ cup "M&M's"® Milk Chocolate Mini Baking Bits into bottoms and sides of dough cups. Preheat oven to 350°F. Bake cookies 8 to 9 minutes. Cookies will be puffy. Remove from oven; gently press down center of each cookie. Return to oven 1 minute. Cool cookies in muffin cups 5 minutes. Remove to wire racks; cool completely. In medium bowl combine water and food coloring. Add coconut; stir until evenly tinted. In each cookie cup, layer 1 teaspoon frosting, 1 teaspoon tinted coconut and 1 teaspoon "M&M's"® Milk Chocolate Mini Baking Bits. Push both licorice ends into frosting to make basket handle. Store in tightly covered container.

*Makes 3 dozen cookies*

**tip**

These little Easter baskets make great place cards for Easter dinner. Write every guests' name on the side of a basket with decorator's frosting.

**Edible Easter Baskets**

# Easter Baskets and Bunnies Cupcakes

- 2 cups sugar
- 1¾ cups all-purpose flour
- ¾ cup HERSHEY'S Cocoa or HERSHEY'S Dutch Processed Cocoa
- 1½ teaspoons baking powder
- 1½ teaspoons baking soda
- 1 teaspoon salt
- 2 eggs
- 1 cup milk
- ½ cup vegetable oil
- 2 teaspoons vanilla extract
- 1 cup boiling water
  Creamy Vanilla Frosting (recipe follows)
  Green, red and yellow food color
- 3¾ cups (10-ounce package) MOUNDS® Sweetened Coconut Flakes, divided and tinted*
  Suggested garnishes (marshmallows, HERSHEY'S MINI KISSES™ Milk Chocolate Baking Pieces, licorice, jelly beans)

*To tint coconut, combine ¾ teaspoon water with several drops green food color in small bowl. Stir in 1¼ cups coconut. Toss with fork until evenly tinted. Repeat with red and yellow food color and remaining coconut.

**1.** Heat oven to 350°F. Line muffin cups (2½ inches in diameter) with paper bake cups.

**2.** Stir together sugar, flour, cocoa, baking powder, baking soda and salt in large bowl. Add eggs, milk, oil and vanilla; beat on medium speed of mixer 2 minutes. Stir in boiling water (batter will be thin). Fill muffin cups ⅔ full with batter.

**3.** Bake 22 to 25 minutes or until wooden pick inserted in center comes out clean. Cool completely. Prepare Creamy Vanilla Frosting; frost cupcakes. Immediately press desired color tinted coconut onto each cupcake. Garnish as desired to resemble Easter basket or bunny.
*Makes about 33 cupcakes*

**Creamy Vanilla Frosting:** Beat ⅓ cup softened butter or margarine in medium bowl. Add 1 cup powdered sugar and 1½ teaspoons vanilla extract; beat well. Add 2½ cups powdered sugar alternately with ¼ cup milk, beating to spreading consistency. Makes about 2 cups frosting.

Easter Baskets and Bunnies Cupcakes

# Patriotic Cocoa Cupcakes

- 2 cups sugar
- 1¾ cups all-purpose flour
- ¾ cup HERSHEY'S Cocoa
- 2 teaspoons baking soda
- 1 teaspoon baking powder
- 1 teaspoon salt
- 2 eggs
- 1 cup buttermilk or sour milk*
- 1 cup boiling water
- ½ cup vegetable oil
- 1 teaspoon vanilla extract
  Vanilla Frosting (recipe follows)
  Chocolate stars or blue and red decorating icing (in tube)

*To sour milk: Use 1 tablespoon white vinegar plus milk to equal 1 cup.

**1.** Heat oven to 350°F. Grease and flour muffin cups (2½-inches in diameter) or line with paper bake cups.

**2.** Combine dry ingredients in large bowl. Add eggs, buttermilk, water, oil and vanilla; beat on medium speed of mixer 2 minutes (batter will be thin). Fill cups ⅔ full with batter.

**3.** Bake 15 minutes or until wooden pick inserted in center comes out clean. Remove cupcakes from pan. Cool completely. To make chocolate stars for garnish, if desired, cut several cupcakes into ½-inch slices; cut out star shapes from cake slices. Frost remaining cupcakes. Garnish with chocolate stars or with blue and red decorating icing.

*Makes about 30 cupcakes*

**Vanilla Frosting:** Beat ¼ cup (½ stick) softened butter, ¼ cup shortening and 2 teaspoons vanilla extract. Add 1 cup powdered sugar; beat until creamy. Add 3 cups powdered sugar alternately with 3 to 4 tablespoons milk, beating to spreading consistency. Makes about 2⅓ cups frosting.

**Patriotic Cocoa Cupcakes**

# Firecrackers

5 cups BAKER'S® ANGEL FLAKE® Coconut
Blue food coloring
24 baked cupcakes, cooled
1 tub (12 ounces) COOL WHIP® Whipped Topping, thawed
Red decorating gel
Red string licorice

**TINT** coconut using blue food coloring.

**TRIM** any "lips" off top edges of cupcakes. Using small amount of whipped topping, attach bottoms of 2 cupcakes together. Repeat with remaining cupcakes. Stand attached cupcakes on 1 end on serving plate or tray.

**FROST** with remaining whipped topping. Press coconut onto sides.

**DRAW** a star on top of each firecracker with decorating gel. Insert pieces of licorice for fuses. Store cakes in refrigerator.

*Makes 12 Firecrackers*

# Black Cat Cupcakes

38 OREO® Chocolate Sandwich Cookies, divided
1 (18¼-ounce) package devil's food cake mix
1 (16-ounce) container chocolate frosting
Black string licorice
Jelly beans
Semi-sweet chocolate chips
Black licorice whip

1. Coarsely chop 14 cookies. Prepare cake mix batter according to package directions; stir in chopped cookies. Spoon batter into 24 (2½-inch) paper-lined muffin cups.

2. Bake at 350°F for 20 minutes or until toothpick inserted in center comes out clean. Remove from pans; cool on wire rack.

3. Decorate the remaining 24 cookies using frosting to attach 4 (1½-inch) licorice strings for whiskers, 2 jelly bean halves for eyes and 2 chocolate chips for ears. Let set at least 30 minutes.

4. Frost cupcakes with remaining frosting. Stand cat faces on edge on each cupcake. Place 3-inch piece licorice whip on back half of each cupcake for tail.    *Makes 24 cupcakes*

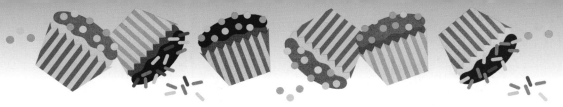

# Witch's Hat Chocolate Cupcakes

• • • • • • • • • • • • • • • •

- ¾ cup (1½ sticks) butter or margarine, softened
- 1⅔ cups sugar
- 3 eggs
- 1 teaspoon vanilla extract
- 2 cups all-purpose flour
- ⅔ cup HERSHEY'S Cocoa
- 1¼ teaspoons baking soda
- 1 teaspoon salt
- ¼ teaspoon baking powder
- 1⅓ cups water
  Orange Cream Filling (recipe follows)

**1.** Heat oven to 350°F. Line muffin cups (2½ inches in diameter) with paper bake cups.

**2.** Combine butter, sugar, eggs and vanilla in large bowl; beat on medium speed of mixer 3 minutes. Stir together flour, cocoa, baking soda, salt and baking powder; add alternately with water to butter mixture, beating after each addition until just blended. Fill muffin cups ⅔ full with batter.

**3.** Bake 20 to 25 minutes or until wooden pick inserted in center comes out clean. Remove from pans to wire racks. Cool completely.

**4.** Prepare Orange Cream Filling. Cut 1½-inch cone-shaped piece from center of each cupcake; reserve. Fill each cavity with scant tablespoon prepared filling. Place reserved cake pieces on filling, pointed side up. Refrigerate before serving. Cover; refrigerate leftover filled cupcakes.

*Makes about 2½ dozen cupcakes*

## Orange Cream Filling

• • • • • • • • • • • • • • • •

- ½ cup (1 stick) butter or margarine, softened
- 1 cup marshmallow creme
- 1¼ cups powdered sugar
- ½ to 1 teaspoon freshly grated orange peel
- ½ teaspoon vanilla extract
- 2 to 3 teaspoons orange juice
  Red and yellow food colors (optional)

**1.** Beat butter in small bowl until creamy; gradually beat in marshmallow creme. Gradually add powdered sugar, orange peel and vanilla, beating until blended. Add orange juice and food colors, if desired; beat until smooth and of desired consistency.

# Boo-tiful Cupcakes

- 24 **Reynolds® Halloween Bake Cups**
- 1 **package (about 18 ounces) cake mix**
- 1 **container (16 ounces) vanilla frosting**
  **Orange food color**
  **Halloween decorator sprinkles**
- 1 **cup premier white morsels**
- 2 **teaspoons shortening (not butter or margarine)**
  **Cut-Rite® Wax Paper**

**PREHEAT** oven to 350°F. Place Reynolds Halloween Bake Cups in muffin pans; set aside. Prepare cake mix following package directions for 24 cupcakes. Spoon batter into bake cups. Bake as directed. Cool.

**TINT** frosting with orange food color; frost cupcakes. Sprinkle with Halloween decorator sprinkles.

**MELT** premier white morsels following package directions. Add shortening; stir until melted. Spoon melted morsels into ghost shapes on cookie sheet lined with Cut-Rite Wax Paper. Use chocolate sprinkles for eyes. Refrigerate until firm. Stand one ghost in center of each cupcake.

*Makes 24 cupcakes*

# Little Devils

- 1 **package (18 ounces) carrot cake mix**
- ½ **cup solid pack pumpkin**
- ⅓ **cup vegetable oil**
- 3 **eggs**
- 1 **container (16 ounces) cream cheese frosting**
  **Assorted Halloween candies, jelly beans, chocolate candies and nuts**

**1.** Preheat oven to 350°F. Prepare cake mix according to package directions, using water as directed on package, pumpkin, oil and eggs. Spoon batter into 18 paper-lined muffin cups. Bake 20 minutes or until toothpick inserted in centers of cupcakes comes out clean. Cool in pans on wire racks 5 minutes; remove and cool completely.

**2.** Frost cupcakes with frosting. Let each goblin guest decorate his own cupcake with assorted candies.

*Makes 18 cupcakes*

**Make-Ahead Time:** up to 3 days in refrigerator or up to 1 month in freezer before serving

**Final Prep Time:** 20 minutes

Boo-tiful Cupcakes

# Scarecrow Cupcakes

- 1¼ cups all-purpose flour
- ¾ teaspoon baking powder
- ½ teaspoon baking soda
- ¼ teaspoon salt
- ¾ teaspoon ground cinnamon
- ⅛ teaspoon ground cloves
- ⅛ teaspoon ground nutmeg
- ⅛ teaspoon ground allspice
- ¾ cup heavy cream
- 2 tablespoons molasses
- ¼ cup butter, softened
- ¼ cup granulated sugar
- ¼ cup packed brown sugar
- 2 eggs
- ½ teaspoon vanilla
- ¾ cup sweetened shredded coconut
  Maple Frosting (recipe follows)
  Toasted coconut, chow mein noodles, shredded wheat cereal, assorted candies and decorator gel

● Preheat oven to 350°F. Line 18 (2¾-inch) muffin cups with paper baking liners. Combine flour, baking powder, baking soda, salt and spices in medium bowl; set aside. Combine cream and molasses in small bowl; set aside.

● Beat butter in large bowl until creamy. Add granulated sugar and brown sugar; beat until light and fluffy. Add eggs, one at a time, beating well after each addition. Blend in vanilla.

● Add flour mixture alternately with cream mixture, beating well after each addition. Stir in coconut; spoon batter into prepared muffin cups, filling about half full.

● Bake 20 to 25 minutes or until toothpick inserted in center comes out clean. Cool in pan on wire rack 10 minutes. Remove cupcakes to racks; cool completely.

● Prepare Maple Frosting. Frost cupcakes and decorate to make scarecrow faces as shown in photo.    *Makes 18 servings*

## Maple Frosting

- 2 tablespoons butter, softened
- 2 tablespoons maple or pancake syrup
- 1½ cups powdered sugar

● Beat butter and syrup in medium bowl until blended. Gradually beat in powdered sugar until smooth.
   *Makes about 1½ cups*

**Scarecrow Cupcakes**

# Merry Santa Cupcakes

24 Reynolds® Holly Bake Cups
1 package (about 18 ounces) white cake mix
1 container (16 ounces) vanilla frosting
Red sugar crystals
Mini candy coated plain chocolate candies
Mini marshmallows
Reynolds® Holiday Prints® Plastic Wrap

**PREHEAT** oven to 350°F. Place Reynolds Holly Bake Cups in muffin pans; set aside. Prepare cake mix following package directions for 24 cupcakes. Spoon batter into bake cups. Bake as directed. Cool.

**FROST** cupcakes. Decorate each cupcake to look like Santa. For hat, sprinkle top third and halfway down one side of cupcake with red sugar crystals. Place chocolate candies on frosting for eyes and nose. Cut 2 marshmallows in half lengthwise, place at edge of red sugar for hat brim. Place a marshmallow at end of red sugar on side for the hat tassel. For beard, place about 9 marshmallows over bottom third of frosting.

**WRAP** cupcakes in Reynolds Holiday Prints Plastic Wrap or place cupcakes in a gift box lined with plastic wrap.

*Makes 24 cupcakes*

## tip

For best results when baking, avoid opening the oven door during the first half of the baking time. The oven temperature must remain constant in order for the cupcakes to rise properly.

Merry Santa Cupcakes

# Reindeer Cupcakes

- 1 package (2-layer size) chocolate cake mix plus ingredients to prepare mix
- ¼ cup (½ stick) butter, softened
- 4 cups powdered sugar
- 5 to 6 tablespoons brewed decaffeinated espresso coffee, divided
- ½ cup (3 ounces) semisweet chocolate chips, melted
- 1 teaspoon vanilla
  Dash salt
- 24 pretzel twists, broken in half
  Assorted candies for decoration

1. Preheat oven to 350°F. Line 24 regular-size (2½-inch) muffin pan cups with paper muffin cup liners.

2. Prepare cake mix according to package directions. Spoon batter into prepared muffin pans. Bake 15 to 20 minutes or until toothpick inserted into centers comes out clean. Cool in pans on wire racks 10 minutes. Remove to racks; cool completely.

3. Beat butter in large bowl with electric mixer at medium speed until creamy. Gradually add powdered sugar and 4 tablespoons coffee; beat until smooth. Beat in melted chocolate, vanilla and salt. Add remaining coffee, 1 tablespoon at a time, until frosting is of desired spreading consistency.

4. Frost cooled cupcakes with frosting. Decorate with broken pretzel pieces for antlers and assorted candies for reindeer faces.      *Makes 24 cupcakes*

### tip

To cut the pretzels into reindeer antlers, use a serrated knife. Gently cut using a back and forth sawing motion without pressing down.

My *Favorites*

# My Favorite Recipes

**Favorite recipe:** _____

**Favorite recipe from:** _____

**Ingredients:** _____

_____

_____

_____

_____

_____

**Method:** _____

_____

_____

_____

_____

_____

_____

_____

_____

_____

_____

**Favorite recipe:** _____

**Favorite recipe from:** _____

**Ingredients:** _____

_____

_____

_____

_____

_____

**Method:** _____

_____

_____

_____

_____

_____

_____

_____

_____

_____

_____

# My Favorite Recipes

Favorite recipe: _____

Favorite recipe from: _____

Ingredients: _____

_____

_____

_____

_____

_____

Method: _____

_____

_____

_____

_____

_____

_____

_____

_____

_____

_____

_____

_____

**Favorite recipe:** _____

**Favorite recipe from:** _____

**Ingredients:** _____

_____

_____

_____

_____

_____

**Method:** _____

_____

_____

_____

_____

_____

_____

_____

_____

_____

_____

_____

# My Favorite Recipes

**Favorite recipe:** _____

**Favorite recipe from:** _____

**Ingredients:** _____

_____

_____

_____

_____

_____

**Method:** _____

_____

_____

_____

_____

_____

_____

_____

_____

_____

_____

_____

**Favorite recipe:** _____

**Favorite recipe from:** _____

**Ingredients:** _____

_____

_____

_____

_____

_____

**Method:** _____

_____

_____

_____

_____

_____

_____

_____

_____

_____

_____

# *My Favorite Recipes*

**Favorite recipe:** _____

**Favorite recipe from:** _____

**Ingredients:** _____

_____

_____

_____

_____

_____

**Method:** _____

_____

_____

_____

_____

_____

_____

_____

_____

_____

_____

**Favorite recipe:** _____

**Favorite recipe from:** _____

**Ingredients:** _____

_____

_____

_____

_____

_____

**Method:** _____

_____

_____

_____

_____

_____

_____

_____

_____

_____

_____

_____

# My Favorite Recipes

Favorite recipe: _____

Favorite recipe from: _____

Ingredients: _____

_____

_____

_____

_____

_____

Method: _____

_____

_____

_____

_____

_____

_____

_____

_____

_____

_____

_____

_____

**Favorite recipe:** _____

**Favorite recipe from:** _____

**Ingredients:** _____

_____

_____

_____

_____

_____

**Method:** _____

_____

_____

_____

_____

_____

_____

_____

_____

_____

_____

_____

_____

# My Favorite Recipes

**Favorite recipe:** _____

**Favorite recipe from:** _____

**Ingredients:** _____

_____

_____

_____

_____

_____

**Method:** _____

_____

_____

_____

_____

_____

_____

_____

_____

_____

_____

_____

**Favorite recipe:** _____

**Favorite recipe from:** _____

**Ingredients:** _____

_____

_____

_____

_____

_____

**Method:** _____

_____

_____

_____

_____

_____

_____

_____

_____

_____

_____

_____

_____

# *My Favorite Recipes*

**Favorite recipe:** _____

**Favorite recipe from:** _____

**Ingredients:** _____

_____

_____

_____

_____

_____

**Method:** _____

_____

_____

_____

_____

_____

_____

_____

_____

_____

_____

_____

# My Favorite Recipes

**Favorite recipe:** _____

**Favorite recipe from:** _____

**Ingredients:** _____

_____

_____

_____

_____

_____

**Method:** _____

_____

_____

_____

_____

_____

_____

_____

_____

_____

_____

_____

# My Favorite Recipes

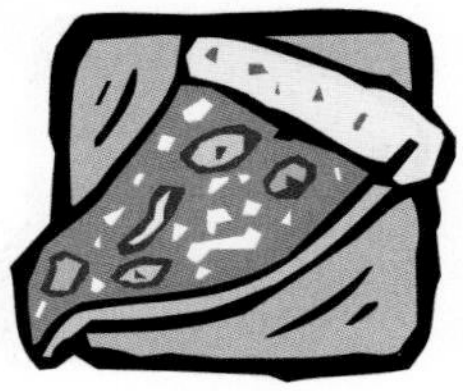

**Favorite recipe:** ______________________________

**Favorite recipe from:** ______________________________

**Ingredients:** ______________________________

______________________________

______________________________

______________________________

______________________________

______________________________

**Method:** ______________________________

______________________________

______________________________

______________________________

______________________________

______________________________

______________________________

______________________________

______________________________

______________________________

______________________________

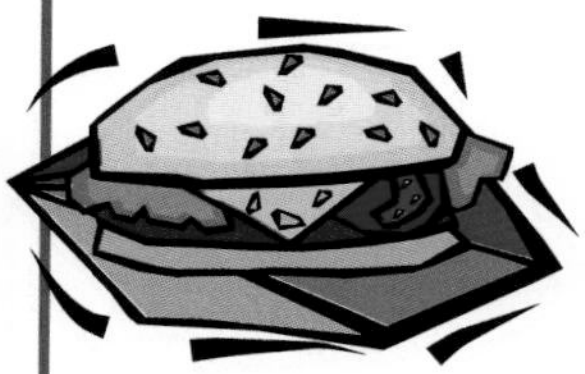

______________________________

______________________________

**Favorite recipe:** _____

**Favorite recipe from:** _____

**Ingredients:** _____

_____

_____

_____

_____

_____

_____

**Method:** _____

_____

_____

_____

_____

_____

_____

_____

_____

_____

_____

_____

_____

_____

# My Favorite Recipes

**Favorite recipe:** _____

**Favorite recipe from:** _____

**Ingredients:** _____

_____

_____

_____

_____

_____

**Method:** _____

_____

_____

_____

_____

_____

_____

_____

_____

_____

_____

_____

_____

## My Favorite Recipes

**Favorite recipe:** _____

**Favorite recipe from:** _____

**Ingredients:** _____

_____

_____

_____

_____

_____

**Method:** _____

_____

_____

_____

_____

_____

_____

_____

_____

_____

_____

_____

_____

# *My Favorite Parties*

**Date:** _____

**What kind of party?** _____
_____

**Who came?** _____
_____
_____
_____
_____

**What did we eat?** _____
_____
_____
_____
_____
_____
_____
_____
_____
_____
_____

**Date:** _____

**What kind of party?** _____

_____

**Who came?** _____

_____

_____

_____

_____

**What did we eat?** _____

_____

_____

_____

_____

_____

_____

_____

_____

_____

_____

# My Favorite Parties

Date: _____

What kind of party? _____

_____

Who came? _____

_____

_____

_____

_____

What did we eat? _____

_____

_____

_____

_____

_____

_____

_____

_____

_____

# My Favorite Parties

Date: _____

What kind of party? _____

_____

Who came? _____

_____

_____

_____

_____

What did we eat? _____

_____

_____

_____

_____

_____

_____

_____

_____

_____

_____

_____

# *My Favorite Parties*

**Date:** _____

**What kind of party?** _____

_____

**Who came?** _____

_____

_____

_____

_____

**What did we eat?** _____

_____

_____

_____

_____

_____

_____

_____

_____

_____

# My Favorite Parties

Date: _____

What kind of party? _____

_____

Who came? _____

_____

_____

_____

_____

What did we eat? _____

_____

_____

_____

_____

_____

_____

_____

_____

_____

_____

# My Favorite Take-Along Treats

Date: _____

Where? _____

Who was there? _____

_____

_____

What did I bring? _____

_____

_____

_____

_____

_____

Date: _____

Where? _____

Who was there? _____

_____

_____

What did I bring? _____

_____

_____

_____

_____

## My Favorite Take-Along Treats

**Date:** _____

**Where?** _____

**Who was there?** _____

_____

_____

**What did I bring?** _____

_____

_____

_____

_____

_____

**Date:** _____

**Where?** _____

**Who was there?** _____

_____

_____

**What did I bring?** _____

_____

_____

_____

_____

266

# My Favorite Take-Along Treats

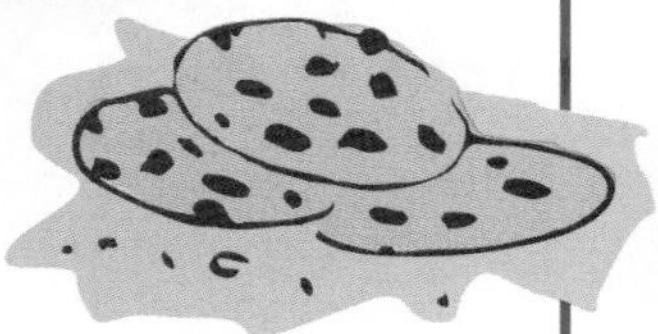

Date: _____

Where? _____

Who was there? _____
_____
_____

What did I bring? _____
_____
_____
_____
_____
_____

Date: _____

Where? _____

Who was there? _____
_____
_____

What did I bring? _____
_____
_____
_____
_____

# My Favorite Take-Along Treats

**Date:** _____

**Where?** _____

**Who was there?** _____

_____

_____

**What did I bring?** _____

_____

_____

_____

_____

_____

**Date:** _____

**Where?** _____

**Who was there?** _____

_____

_____

**What did I bring?** _____

_____

_____

_____

_____

# My Favorite Friends

**Friend:** _____

**They love:** _____

_____

_____

**They don't like:** _____

_____

_____

**Friend:** _____

**They love:** _____

_____

_____

**They don't like:** _____

_____

_____

**Friend:** _____

**They love:** _____

_____

_____

**They don't like:** _____

_____

_____

# My Favorite Friends

**Friend:** _____

**They love:** _____

_____

_____

**They don't like:** _____

_____

_____

**Friend:** _____

**They love:** _____

_____

_____

**They don't like:** _____

_____

_____

**Friend:** _____

**They love:** _____

_____

_____

**They don't like:** _____

_____

_____

270

# My Favorite Friends

**Friend:** _____

**They love:** _____

_____

_____

**They don't like:** _____

_____

_____

**Friend:** _____

**They love:** _____

_____

_____

**They don't like:** _____

_____

_____

**Friend:** _____

**They love:** _____

_____

_____

**They don't like:** _____

_____

_____

271

# My Favorite Friends

**Friend:** _____

**They love:** _____

_____

_____

**They don't like:** _____

_____

_____

**Friend:** _____

**They love:** _____

_____

_____

**They don't like:** _____

_____

_____

**Friend:** _____

**They love:** _____

_____

_____

**They don't like:** _____

_____

_____

# Hints, Tips & Index

# Kids Make Cooking Fun

*Kids are loads of fun . . . and a bit of work! Luckily, cooking for them can be one of the fun aspects. All you need are simple recipes for nutritious foods that look good and taste yummy. If food is interesting and appealing, the kids will love it.*

## Cooking for Kids

Cooking for kids can be a great family event, both when the food's prepared and when it's eaten. Family meals are a healthful alternative to the "grab anything" foods that kids often eat. It's a great way to bring everyone together and discuss the day's events.

These recipes offer a variety of meal options that are sure to please and entertain. Today's families are busier than ever, so you can choose from many recipes that can be prepared quickly. Use the recipes for sweets and parties to create special events your children's friends can enjoy, too.

You'll also find recipes to help you whip up fast, tempting treats for snack time. Making homemade snacks for school or playtime encourages kids to develop good eating habits. It also discourages them from buying convenience snacks from machines.

## Cooking with Kids

Kids feel very special when their parents cook up delightful goodies just for them. And helping out in the kitchen can make the experience even more fun. In fact, some professionals believe that cooking is as educational as it is exciting for children.

Helping to cook involves several valuable skills important to child development:

● Planning a series of steps in a process

● Using mathematical skills to measure ingredients and time the cooking of foods

● Reading and interpreting written instructions used in recipes

● Expanding creative boundaries

● Mastering teamwork when cooking with adults and other children

Use your judgement to decide when your kids might be able to help out. Consider their interest, experience in the kitchen, level of responsibility, ability to focus on tasks and follow written recipes and verbal instructions. You know them better than anyone, so your experience should be your guide.

273

# Kids Make Cooking Fun

## Keep Little Helpers Safe

Your little helpers can have lots of fun helping with the cooking. It can be very exciting, and they'll be proud to share what they helped make. But take time to introduce them to good kitchen habits so no one gets hurt.

Explain the rules regarding kitchen appliances (rangetop, oven, microwave oven, etc.) and implements (sharp knives, food processors, blenders, mixers, etc.) that only adults will use. Also, discuss what to do in case a spill or break occurs. The kids should feel confident that grown-up supervision and help are always there if needed.

Remember, some things we take for granted as adults can be a bit challenging for little ones. For instance, you'll need to reach items on high shelves, handle large or heavy objects and use adult-sized implements or even pot holders. Make sure you keep pots and pans away from the edge of the counter or stove to avoid spills and burns.

## Let's Get Cooking!

Having the kids assist can be a great help to parents. Extra hands can lighten the load of preparing meals and cleaning up afterwards. And you might get more menu suggestions from your little ones, easing your task of constantly thinking up new and different meal ideas.

But most of all, you'll find that time spent with kids in the kitchen brings the family closer together, creates quality time for all and offers many opportunities for fun and learning. Now that you're all ready...get cooking for kids!

# Great Parties for Great Kids

*For any party, whether it's a small birthday party for a child and some friends or a huge holiday gathering that includes kids, planning is the key to making things go smoothly and seeing that everyone has a good time.*

## Planning a Party

Long before the event, give thought to the mood and look you want the party to have. Ask yourself some questions, then discuss them with the child and other participants. Put ideas down on paper, as this helps to avoid confusion later on.

Will the event use many decorations or should it be very simple in design? If the event is for a holiday such as Thanksgiving or Christmas, will there be a traditional look and menu, or would you prefer a special theme? For a non-holiday party, such as a birthday, is there a theme for the event? For instance, if the birthday boy or girl is a fan of car racing or a certain cartoon character, what decorating options could you include to reflect the theme? Plates and napkins, balloons and small gifts could greatly enhance the feel of the party.

Keep your budget in mind. A smaller budget might mean the kids could design, make and send out the invitations themselves. They can also make streamers and table decorations, either at the party as a group activity or ahead of time. Perhaps your guests could contribute by bringing a special dish; have suggestions ready if you plan this, as they might ask about your preferences.

## Planning Party Menus

Your budget will also influence the number of guests to invite and the type and quantity of items you will cook. Do you want an entire meal, or snacks and desserts? Sit down and plan out the menu. Use the following guidelines to help plan your menu:

● Select the main dish first, then plan the other dishes around it.

● Include different colors, textures and types of food to add excitement. Imagine the foods on the table and on a plate, and add foods that are fun, like crunchy vegetables and dippers.

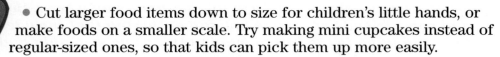

- Cut larger food items down to size for children's little hands, or make foods on a smaller scale. Try making mini cupcakes instead of regular-sized ones, so that kids can pick them up more easily.

- Keep it simple where possible. If you're preparing several very involved or time-consuming dishes, be sure the side dishes and extras don't require a lot of work. You might want to purchase the cake, bread or other items that take longer to make.

- After selecting menu items, estimate the time needed for preparing each one. Plan when to start cooking each item, and who will be assisting with each part of the event, including the serving of each course or food.

- Choose recipes that can be prepared ahead of time; if some parts can be made ahead and stored in the refrigerator or freezer, it puts less pressure on you as host.

- Review all of the recipes ahead of time, then prepare a comprehensive shopping list. Remember to place any special orders well in advance. Buy nonperishable ingredients ahead of time; perishable foods can be bought close to the time of the party.

- Double-check your lists and supplies beforehand, so that you won't have to run out for last-minute items. Ask guests to bring any critical things you might have forgotten.

Be sure to include the kids in as many of the steps as possible; ask them what they want to do and determine what game plan you all feel comfortable with. Then, stick to it . . . and have a great party!

# Cooking Terms

**Baste:** The technique of brushing, spooning or pouring liquids over food, usually meat and poultry, as it cooks to preserve moistness and add flavor.

**Blanch:** Cooking foods, most often vegetables, briefly in boiling water and quickly cooling in cold water, either to remove the skin or extend shelf life.

**Cut In:** Combining a solid fat, such as butter, with dry ingredients, using two knives or a pastry blender until the mixture is in coarse, small pieces.

**Deglaze:** Retrieving flavorful bits of food after meat has been browned. While the pan is still hot, add a small amount of liquid; stir to loosen browned bits.

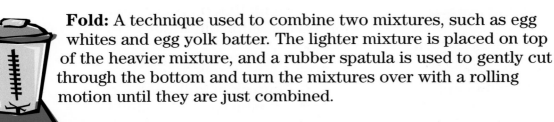

**Fold:** A technique used to combine two mixtures, such as egg whites and egg yolk batter. The lighter mixture is placed on top of the heavier mixture, and a rubber spatula is used to gently cut through the bottom and turn the mixtures over with a rolling motion until they are just combined.

**Poach:** The technique of cooking food slowly and gently in a simmering, not boiling, liquid that just covers the food.

**Purée:** To mash or strain a food until it is smooth, either with a food processor, sieve, blender or food mill.

**Reduce:** To boil a liquid, usually a sauce, until its volume has been decreased through evaporation, resulting in a more intense flavor.

**Sauté:** To rapidly cook or brown food in a small amount of fat in a skillet.

**Simmer:** Cooking a liquid or a food in a liquid with gentle heat just below the boiling point, so that tiny bubbles rise to the surface.

**Whisk:** Stirring, whipping or beating foods with a wire whisk.

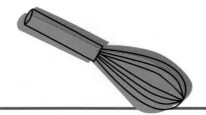

# How Much of This=That?

| If you don't have: | Use: |
| --- | --- |
| 1 cup buttermilk | 1 tablespoon lemon juice or vinegar plus milk to equal 1 cup (stir; let stand 5 minutes) |
| 1 tablespoon cornstarch | 2 tablespoons all-purpose flour or 2 teaspoons arrowroot |
| 1 cup beef or chicken broth | 1 bouillon cube or 1 teaspoon granules mixed with 1 cup boiling water |
| 1 small clove garlic | ⅛ teaspoon garlic powder |
| 1 tablespoon prepared mustard | 1 teaspoon dry mustard |
| 1 cup tomato sauce | ½ cup tomato paste plus ½ cup cold water |
| 1 teaspoon vinegar | 2 teaspoons lemon juice |
| 1 cup whole milk | 1 cup skim milk plus 2 tablespoons melted butter |
| 1 cup sour cream | 1 cup plain yogurt |

## Common Weights and Measures

Dash = less than ⅛ teaspoon

½ tablespoon = 1½ teaspoons

1 tablespoon = 3 teaspoons

2 tablespoons = ⅛ cup

¼ cup = 4 tablespoons

⅓ cup = 5 tablespoons plus 1 teaspoon

½ cup = 8 tablespoons

¾ cup = 12 tablespoons

1 cup = 16 tablespoons

½ pint = 1 cup or 8 fluid ounces

1 pint = 2 cups or 16 fluid ounces

1 quart = 4 cups or 2 pints or 32 fluid ounces

1 gallon = 16 cups or 4 quarts

1 pound = 16 ounces

# Baking Basics

- Read the entire recipe before you begin to be sure you have all the necessary ingredients and utensils.

- Remove butter, margarine and cream cheese from the refrigerator to soften, if necessary.

- Adjust oven racks and preheat the oven. Check oven temperature with an oven thermometer to make sure the temperature is accurate.

- Toast and chop nuts and melt butter and chocolate before preparing batter or dough.

- Always use the pan size suggested in the recipe. Prepare pans as directed.

- Choose cookie sheets that fit in your oven with at least 1 inch on all sides between the edge of the sheet and the oven wall.

- Grease cookie sheets only when the recipe recommends it; otherwise, the cookies may spread too much.

- Measure the ingredients accurately and assemble them in the order they are listed in the recipe.

- When baking more than one sheet of cookies at a time, it's best to rotate them for even baking. Halfway through the baking time, rotate the cookie sheets from front to back as well as from the top rack to the bottom rack.

- Always check for doneness at the minimum baking time given in the recipe.

# Is it Done Yet?

Use the following guides to test for doneness.

### CASEROLES

until hot and bubbly
until heated through
until cheese melts

### MEAT

#### Beef
medium    140°F to 145°F
well done 160°F

#### Veal
medium    145°F to 150°F
well done 160°F

#### Lamb
medium    145°F
well done 160°F

#### Pork
well done 165°F to 170°F

### POULTRY

#### Chicken
until temperature in thigh
   is 180°F (whole bird)
until chicken is no longer
   pink in center
until temperature in breast
   is 170°F

### SEAFOOD

#### Fish
until fish begins to flake
   against the grain when
   tested with fork

#### Shrimp
until shrimp are pink and
   opaque

### SAUCES
until (slightly) thickened

### SOUPS
until heated through

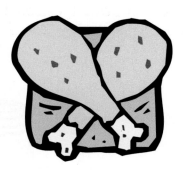

### STEWS
until meat is tender
until vegetables are tender

### VEGETABLES
until crisp-tender
until tender
until browned

# Gift-Giving Tips

## THE PERFECT PACKAGE

Homemade gifts are made extraordinary when tucked into unique packages lavished with decorative accessories.

**Airtight Canisters:** These containers are available in a variety of materials, including glass and plastic. They are great for storing snack mixes, cookies and candies.

**Baskets:** These versatile hold-alls are available in a wide variety of materials and sizes. Large, sturdy ones are well-suited for packing entire gift themes. Oblong shapes are great for breads, and smaller types are just right for cookies and candies.

**Boxes:** Boxes come in all shapes and sizes and are good for packaging cookies, candies, breads and truffles.

**Glass Bottles:** Airtight bottles are perfect for barbecue or other types of sauces. Always choose securely stoppered bottles to help prevent leakage.

**Glass Jars:** Jars are wonderful for presenting mustards, chutneys and snack mixes. Make sure the jar has an airtight lid.

**Gift Bags:** These handy totes come in a wide variety of sizes and colors. Pack individual cookies and candies in smaller bags; package goodie-filled jars or canisters in larger bags.

**Tins:** Metal containers with tight-fitting lids are just the right thing for snack mixes, cookies, candies and truffles. They also hold up well when sent through the mail.

# *Metric Conversion Chart*

## VOLUME MEASUREMENTS (dry)

⅛ teaspoon = 0.5 mL
¼ teaspoon = 1 mL
½ teaspoon = 2 mL
¾ teaspoon = 4 mL
1 teaspoon = 5 mL
1 tablespoon = 15 mL
2 tablespoons = 30 mL
¼ cup = 60 mL
⅓ cup = 75 mL
½ cup = 125 mL
⅔ cup = 150 mL
¾ cup = 175 mL
1 cup = 250 mL
2 cups = 1 pint = 500 mL
3 cups = 750 mL
4 cups = 1 quart = 1 L

## VOLUME MEASUREMENTS (fluid)

1 fluid ounce (2 tablespoons) = 30 mL
4 fluid ounces (½ cup) = 125 mL
8 fluid ounces (1 cup) = 250 mL
12 fluid ounces (1½ cups) = 375 mL
16 fluid ounces (2 cups) = 500 mL

## WEIGHTS (mass)

½ ounce = 15 g
1 ounce = 30 g
3 ounces = 90 g
4 ounces = 120 g
8 ounces = 225 g
10 ounces = 285 g
12 ounces = 360 g
16 ounces = 1 pound = 450 g

## DIMENSIONS

1/16 inch = 2 mm
⅛ inch = 3 mm
¼ inch = 6 mm
½ inch = 1.5 cm
¾ inch = 2 cm
1 inch = 2.5 cm

## OVEN TEMPERATURES

250°F = 120°C
275°F = 140°C
300°F = 150°C
325°F = 160°C
350°F = 180°C
375°F = 190°C
400°F = 200°C
425°F = 220°C
450°F = 230°C

## BAKING PAN SIZES

| Utensil | Size in Inches/Quarts | Metric Volume | Size in Centimeters |
|---|---|---|---|
| Baking or Cake Pan (square or rectangular) | 8×8×2 | 2 L | 20×20×5 |
| | 9×9×2 | 2.5 L | 23×23×5 |
| | 12×8×2 | 3 L | 30×20×5 |
| | 13×9×2 | 3.5 L | 33×23×5 |
| Loaf Pan | 8×4×3 | 1.5 L | 20×10×7 |
| | 9×5×3 | 2 L | 23×13×7 |
| Round Layer Cake Pan | 8×1½ | 1.2 L | 20×4 |
| | 9×1½ | 1.5 L | 23×4 |
| Pie Plate | 8×1¼ | 750 mL | 20×3 |
| | 9×1¼ | 1 L | 23×3 |
| Baking Dish or Casserole | 1 quart | 1 L | — |
| | 1½ quart | 1.5 L | — |
| | 2 quart | 2 L | — |

# *Acknowledgments*

**The publisher would like to thank the companies and organizations listed below for the use of their recipes and photographs in this publication.**

Birds Eye®

Bob Evans®

California Dried Plum Board

Campbell Soup Company

Cherry Marketing Institute

Duncan Hines® and Moist Deluxe® are
registered trademarks of Aurora Foods Inc.

Eagle® Brand

The Golden Grain Company®

Hebrew National®

Hershey Foods Corporation

Kraft Foods Holdings

Lawry's® Foods, Inc.

Unilever Bestfoods North America

©Mars, Inc. 2002

National Honey Board

Nestlé USA, Inc.

OREO® Chocolate Sandwich Cookies

The Proctor & Gamble Company

Reckitt Benckiser

Reynolds Metals Company

The J.M. Smucker Company

USA Rice Federation

# Index

# *Index*

# Index